Linguistic pr
in sociocultur
practice

Gunther Kress

6–7 Defining discourse 12 Defining texts 18 Language always happens as texts. 19 Defining genres. 39 The construction of a reader position has 2 effects 47 The function of a writer is as an assembler of texts rather than as a creator of texts 53 Tag question 57 The strategy of retreat. 73 Ideologies determine the arrangements of discourses in a text.

Series Editor: Frances Christie

Oxford University Press
1989

Oxford University Press
Walton Street, Oxford OX2 6DP

Oxford   New York   Toronto
Delhi   Bombay   Calcutta   Madras   Karachi
Petaling Jaya   Singapore   Hong Kong   Tokyo
Nairobi   Dar es Salaam   Cape Town
Melbourne   Auckland

and associated companies in
Berlin   Ibadan

Oxford English and the *Oxford English* logo are trade marks of
Oxford University Press

ISBN 019 437156 5

© Deakin University 1985, 1989

First published 1985
Second edition 1989

Printed in Hong Kong.

About the author

Gunther Kress

Gunther Kress thinks that the two major events that have shaped his academic interests are learning a second culture and language in late teenage, and being a student of Michael Halliday's in his mid-twenties. He knows that he has recovered from neither. Consequently his academic work has increasingly been in the area of culture and language, and that is reflected in his major publications. These are (as editor) *Halliday: System and Function in Language*, Oxford University Press, 1976;  *Communication and Culture*, University of New South Wales Press, 1987; (as co-author and author) *Language as Ideology, Language and Control*, both Routledge and Kegan Paul, 1979; *Literature, Language and Society in England 1580-1680*, Macmillan, 1982; *Learning to Write*, Routledge and Kegan Paul, 1982; *Social Semiotics*, Polity, 1988. He explains his interest in language in education as a particular example of the interrelation of culture and language, a fundamentally important one. He is currently Professor of Communications at the University of Technology, Sydney.

Foreword

In a sense, educational interest in language is not new. Studies of rhetoric and of grammar go back as far as the Greeks; in the English-speaking countries, studies of the classical languages, and more recently of English itself, have had a well established place in educational practice. Moreover, a number of the issues which have aroused the most passionate debates about how to develop language abilities have tended to remain, resurfacing at various points in history in somewhat different formulations perhaps, but nonetheless still there, and still lively.

Of these issues, probably the most lively has been that concerning the extent to which explicit knowledge about language on the part of the learner is a desirable or a useful thing. But the manner in which discussion about this issue has been conducted has often been allowed to obscure other and bigger questions: questions, for example, both about the nature of language as an aspect of human experience, and about language as a resource of fundamental importance in the building of human experience. The tendency in much of the western intellectual tradition has been to dissociate language and experience, in such a way that language is seen as rather neutral, merely serving to 'carry' the fruits of experience. Whereas in this view language is seen as a kind of 'conduit', subservient to experience in various ways, an alternative view, as propounded in the books in this series, would argue that language is itself not only a part of experience, but intimately involved in the manner in which we construct and organise experience. As such, it is never neutral, but deeply implicated in building meaning. One's notions concerning how to teach about language will differ quite markedly, depending upon the view one adopts concerning language and experience. In fact, though discussions concerning teaching about language can sometimes be interesting, in practice many such discussions have proved theoretically ill-founded and barren, serving merely to perpetuate a number of unhelpful myths about language.

The most serious and confusing of these myths are those which would suggest we can dissociate language from meaning — form from function, or form from 'content'. Where such myths apply, teaching about language becomes a matter of teaching about 'language rules' — normally grammatical rules — and as history has demonstrated over the years, such teaching rapidly degenerates into the arid pursuit of parts of speech and the parsing of isolated sentences. Meaning, and the critical role of language in the building of meaning, are simply overlooked, and the kinds of knowledge about language made available to the learner are of a very limited kind.

The volumes in this series of monographs devoted to language education in my view provide a much better basis upon which to address questions related to the teaching about language than has been the case anywhere in the English-speaking world for some time now. I make this claim for several reasons, one of the most important being that the series never sought directly to establish a model for teaching about language at all. On the contrary, it sought to establish a principled model of language, which, once properly articulated, allows us to address many questions of an educational nature, including those to do with teaching about language. To use Halliday's term (1978), such a model sees language primarily as a 'social semiotic', and as a resource for meaning, centrally involved in the processes by which human beings negotiate, construct and change the nature of social experience. While the series certainly does not claim to have had the last word on these and related subjects, I believe it does do much to set a new educational agenda — one which enables us to look closely at the role of language both in living and in learning: one which, moreover, provides a basis upon which to decide those kinds of teaching and learning about language which may make a legitimate contribution to the development of the learner.

I have said that arguments to do with teaching about language have been around for a long time: certainly as long as the two hundred years of white settlement in Australia. In fact, coincidentally, just as the first settlers were taking up their enforced residence in the Australian colony of New South Wales, Lindley Murray was preparing his *English Grammar* (1795), which, though not the only volume produced on the subject in the eighteenth century, was certainly the best. Hundreds of school grammars that were to appear in Britain and Australia for the next century at least, were to draw very heavily upon what Murray had written. The parts of speech, parsing and sentence analysis, the latter as propounded by Morell (an influential inspector of schools in England), were the principal elements in the teaching about language in the Australian colonies, much as they were in England throughout the century. By the 1860s and 1870s the Professor of Classics and Logic at Sydney University, Charles Badham, who had arrived from England in 1867, publicly disagreed with the examining authorities in New South Wales concerning the teaching of grammar. To the contemporary reader there is a surprising modernity about many of his objections, most notably his strongly held conviction that successful control of one's language is learned less as a matter of committing to memory the parts of speech and the principles of parsing, than as a matter of frequent opportunity for use.

Historically, the study by which issues of use had been most effectively addressed had been that of rhetoric, in itself quite old in the English-speaking tradition, dating back at least to the sixteenth century. Rhetorical studies flourished in the eighteenth century, the best known works on the subject being George Campbell's *The Philosophy of Rhetoric* (1776), and Hugh Blair's *Lectures on Rhetoric and Belles Lettres* (1783), while in the nineteenth century Richard Whately published his work, *Elements of Rhetoric* (1828). As the nineteenth century proceeded, scholarly work on rhetoric declined, as was testified by the markedly inferior but nonetheless influential works of Alexander Bain (*English Composition and Rhetoric*, 1866; Revised version, 1887). Bain, in fact, did much to corrupt and destroy the older rhetorical traditions, primarily because he lost sight of the need for a basic concern with meaning in language. Bain's was the century of romanticism after all: on the one hand, Matthew Arnold was extolling the civilising influence of English literature in the development of children; on the other hand, there was a tendency towards suspicion, even contempt, for those who wanted to take a scholarly look at the linguistic organisation of texts, and at the ways in which they were structured for the building of meaning. In 1921, Ballard (who was an expert witness before the Newbolt Enquiry on the teaching of English), wrote a book called *Teaching the Mother Tongue*, in which he noted among other things, that unfortunately in England at least rhetorical studies had become associated with what were thought to be rather shallow devices for persuasion and argument. The disinclination to take seriously the study of the rhetorical organisation of texts gave rise to a surprisingly unhelpful tradition for the teaching of literature, which is with us yet in many places: 'civilising' it might be, but it was *not* to be the object of systematic study, for such study would in some ill-defined way threaten or devalue the work of literature itself.

A grammarian like Murray had never been in doubt about the relationship of grammar and rhetoric. As he examined it, grammar was concerned with the syntax of the written English sentence: it was not concerned with the study of 'style', about which he wrote a short appendix in his original grammar, where his debt to the major rhetoricians of the period was apparent. Rhetorical studies, especially as discussed by Campbell for instance, did address questions of 'style', always from the standpoint of a recognition of the close relationship of language to the socially created purpose in using language. In fact, the general model of language as discussed by Campbell bore some relationship to the model taken up in this series, most notably in its commitment to register.

The notion of register proposes a very intimate relationship of text to context: indeed, so intimate is that relationship, it is asserted, that the one can only be interpreted by reference to the other. Meaning is realised in language (in the form of text), which is thus shaped or patterned in response to the context of situation in which it is used. To study language then, is to concentrate upon exploring how it is systematically patterned towards important social ends. The linguistic theory adopted here is that of systemic linguistics. Such a linguistic theory is itself also a social theory, for it proposes firstly, that it is in the nature of human behaviour to build reality and/or experience through complex semiotic processes, and secondly, that the principal semiotic system available to humans is their language. In this sense, to study language is to explore some of the most important and pervasive of the processes by which human beings build their world.

I originally developed the volumes in this series as the basis of two major off campus courses in Language Education taught in the Master's degree program at Deakin University, Victoria, Australia. To the best of my knowledge, such courses, which are designed primarily for teachers and teacher educators, are the first of their kind in the world, and while they actually appeared in the mid 1980s, they emerge from work in language education which has been going on in Australia for some time. This included the national Language Development Project, to which Michael Halliday was consultant, and whose work I co-ordinated throughout its second, productive phase. (This major project was initiated by the Commonwealth Government's Curriculum Development Centre, Canberra, in the 1970s, and involved the co-operation of curriculum development teams from all Australian states in developing language curriculum materials. Its work was not completed because of political changes which caused the activities of the Curriculum Development Centre to be wound down.) In the 1980s a number of conferences have been held fairly regularly in different parts of Australia, all of them variously exploring aspects of language education, and leading to the publication of a number of conference reports. They include: Frances Christie (ed.), *Language and the Social Construction of Experience* (Deakin University, 1983); Brendan Bartlett and John Carr (eds.), *Language in Education Workshop: a Report of Proceedings* (Centre for Research and Learning, Brisbane C.A.E., Mount Gravatt Campus, Brisbane, 1984); Ruqaiya Hasan (ed.), *Discourse on Discourse* (Applied Linguistics Association of Australia, Occasional Papers, Number 7, 1985); Clare Painter and J.R. Martin (eds.), *Writing to Mean: Teaching Genres across the Curriculum* (Applied Linguistics Association of Australia, Occasional Papers, Number 9, 1986); Linda Gerot, Jane Oldenburg and Theo Van Leeuwen (eds.), *Language and Socialisation: Home and School* (in preparation). All these activities have contributed to the building of a climate of opinion and a tradition of thinking about language which made possible the development of the volumes in this series.

While it is true that the developing tradition of language education which these volumes represent does, as I have noted, take up some of the concerns of the older rhetorical studies, it nonetheless also looks forward, pointing to ways of examining language which were not available in earlier times. For example, the notion of language as a social semiotic, and its associated conception of experience or reality as socially built and constantly subject to processes of transformation, finds very much better expression today than would have been possible before, though obviously much more requires to be said about this than can be dealt with in these volumes. In addition, a functionally driven view of language is now available, currently most completely articulated in Halliday's *An Introduction to Functional Grammar* (1985), which offers ways of understanding the English language in a manner that Murray's Grammar could not have done.

Murray's Grammar confined itself to considerations of the syntax of the written English sentence. It did not have anything of use to say about spoken language, as opposed to written language, and, equally, it provided no basis upon which to explore a unit other than the sentence, whether that be the paragraph, or, even more importantly, the total text. The preoccupation with the written sentence reflected the pre-eminent position being accorded to the written word by Murray's time, leading to disastrous consequences since, that is the diminished value accorded to spoken language, especially in educational practices. In Murray's work, the lack of a direct relationship between the study of grammar on the one hand, and that of 'style', on the other hand, was, as I have already noted, to be attributed to his view that it was the rhetorician who addressed wider questions relating to the text. In the tradition in which he worked, in fact, grammar looked at syntactic rules divorced from considerations of meaning or social purpose.

By contrast, Halliday's approach to grammar has a number of real strengths, the first of which is the fact that its basis is semantic, not syntactic: that is to say, it is a semantically driven grammar, which, while not denying that certain principles of syntax do apply, seeks to consider and identify the role of various linguistic items in any text in terms of their function in building meaning. It is for this reason that its practices for interpreting and labelling various linguistic items and groupings are functionally based, not syntactically based. There is in other words, no dissociation of 'grammar' on the one hand and 'semantics' or meaning on the other. A second strength of Halliday's approach is that it is not uniquely interested in written language, being instead committed to the study of both the spoken and written modes, and to an explanation of the differences between the two, in such a way that each is illuminated because of its contrast with the other. A third and final strength of the systemic functional grammar is that it permits useful movement across the text, addressing the manner in which linguistic patternings are built up for the construction of the overall text in its particular 'genre', shaped as it is in response to the context of situation which gave rise to it.

Halliday's functional grammar lies behind all ten volumes in this series, though one other volume, by Michael Christie, called *Aboriginal perspectives on experience and learning: the role of language in Aboriginal Education*, draws upon somewhat different if still compatible perspectives in educational and language theory to develop its arguments. The latter volume, is available directly from Deakin University. In varying ways, the volumes in this series provide a helpful introduction to much that is more fully dealt with in Halliday's Grammar, and I commend the series to the reader who wants to develop some sense of the ways such a body of linguistic theory can be applied to educational questions. A version of the grammar specifically designed for teacher education remains to be written, and while I cherish ambitions to begin work on such a version soon, I am aware that others have similar ambitions − in itself a most desirable development.

While I have just suggested that the reader who picks up any of the volumes in this series should find ways to apply systemic linguistic theory to educational theory, I want to argue, however, that what is offered here is more than merely a course in applied linguistics, legitimate though such a course might be. Rather, I want to claim that this is a course in educational linguistics, a term of importance because it places linguistic study firmly at the heart of educational enquiry. While it is true that a great deal of linguistic research of the past, where it did not interpret language in terms of interactive, social processes, or where it was not grounded in a concern for meaning, has had little of relevance to offer education, socially relevant traditions of linguistics like that from which systemics is derived, do have a lot to contribute. How that contribution should be articulated is quite properly a matter of development in partnership between educationists, teachers and linguistics, and a great deal has yet to be done to achieve such articulation.

I believe that work in Australia currently is making a major contribution to the development of a vigorous educational linguistics, not all of it of course in a systemic framework. I would note here the important work of such people as J.R. Martin, Joan Rothery, Suzanne Eggins and Peter Wignell of the University of Sydney, investigating children's writing development; the innovatory work of Brian Gray and his colleagues a few years ago in developing language programs for Aboriginal children in central Australia, and more recently his work with other groups in Canberra; the recent work of Beth Graham, Michael Christie and Stephen Harris, all of the Northern Territory Department of Education, in developing language programs for Aboriginal children; the important work of John Carr and his colleagues of the Queensland Department of Education in developing new perspectives upon language in the various language curriculum guidelines they have prepared for their state; the contributions of Jenny Hammond of the University of Wollongong, New South Wales, in her research into language development in schools, as well as the various programs in which she teaches; research being undertaken by Ruqaiya Hasan and Carmel Cloran of Macquarie University, Sydney, into children's language learning styles in the transition years from home to school; investigations by Linda Gerot, also of Macquarie University, into classroom discourse in the secondary school, across a number of different subjects; and the work of Pam Gilbert of James Cook University, Townsville, in Queensland, whose interests are both in writing in the secondary school, and in language and gender.

The signs are that a coherent educational linguistics is beginning to appear around the world, and I note with pleasure the appearance of two new and valuable international journals: *Language and Education*, edited by David Corson of Massey University, New Zealand, and *Linguistics in Education*, edited by David Bloome, of the University of Massachusetts. Both are committed to the development of an educational linguistics, to which many traditions of study, linguistic, semiotic and sociological, will no doubt make an important contribution. Such an educational linguistics is long overdue, and in what are politically difficult times, I suggest such a study can make a major contribution to the pursuit of educational equality of opportunity, and to attacking the wider social problems of equity and justice. Language is a political institution: those who are wise in its ways, capable of using it to shape and serve important personal and social goals, will be the ones who are 'empowered' (to use a fashionable word): able, that is, not merely to participate effectively *in* the world, but able also *to act upon it*, in the sense that they can strive for significant social change. Looked at in these terms, provision of appropriate language education programs is a profoundly important matter, both in ensuring equality of educational opportunity, and in helping to develop those who are able and willing to take an effective role in democratic processes of all kinds.

One of the most encouraging measures of the potential value of the perspectives open to teachers taking up an educational linguistics of the kind offered in these monographs, has been the variety of teachers attracted to the courses of which they form a part, and the ways in which these teachers have used what they have learned in undertaking research papers for the award of the master's degree. They include, for example, secondary teachers of physics, social science, geography and English, specialists in teaching English as a second language to migrants and specialists in teaching English to Aboriginal people, primary school teachers, a nurse educator, teachers of illiterate adults, and language curriculum consultants, as well as a number of teacher educators with specialist responsibilities in teaching language education. For many of these people the perspectives offered by an educational linguistics are both new and challenging, causing them to review and change aspects of their teaching practices in various ways. Coming to terms with a semantically driven grammar is in itself quite demanding, while there is often considerable effort involved to bring to conscious awareness the ways in which we use language for the realisation of different meanings. But the effort is plainly worth it, principally because of the added sense of control and direction it can give teachers interested to work at fostering and developing students who are independent and confident in using language for the achievement of various goals. Those people for whom these books have proved helpful, tend to say that they have achieved a stronger and richer appreciation of language and how it works than they had before; that because they know considerably more about language themselves, they are able to intervene much more effectively in directing and guiding those whom they teach; that because they have a better sense of the relationship of language and 'content' than they had before, they can better guide their students into control of the 'content' of the various subjects for which they are responsible; and finally, that because they have an improved sense of how to direct language learning, they are able to institute new assessment policies, negotiating, defining and clarifying realistic goals for their students. By any standards, these are considerable achievements.

As I draw this Foreword to a close, I should perhaps note for the reader's benefit the manner in which students doing course work with me are asked to read the monographs in this series, though I should stress that the books were deliberately designed to be picked up and read in any order one likes. In the first of the two semester courses, called *Language and Learning*, students are asked to read the following volumes in the order given:

Frances Christie — *Language education*
Clare Painter — *Learning the mother tongue*
M.A.K. Halliday & Ruqaiya Hasan — *Language, context, and
   text: aspects of language in a social-semiotic perspective*
J.L. Lemke — *Using language in the classroom*
then either,
M.A.K. Halliday — *Spoken and written language*
or,
Ruqaiya Hasan — *Linguistics, language, and verbal art.*

The following four volumes, together with the one by Michael Christie, mentioned above, belong to the second course called *Sociocultural Aspects of Language and Education*, and they may be read by the students in any order they like, though only three of the five need be selected for close study:

David Butt — *Talking and thinking: the patterns of
   behaviour*
Gunther Kress — *Linguistic processes in sociocultural practice*
J.R. Martin — *Factual writing: exploring and challenging
   social reality*
Cate Poynton — *Language and gender: making the difference*

References

Bain, A., *An English Grammar* (Longman, Roberts and Green, London, 1863).

Bain, A., *English Composition and Rhetoric*, revised in two Parts — *Part 1, Intellectual Elements of Style*, and *Part 11, Emotional Qualities of Style* (Longman, Green and Company, London, 1887).

Ballard, P., *Teaching the Mother Tongue* (Hodder & Stoughton, London, 1921).

Blair, H., *Lectures on Rhetoric and Belles Lettres, Vols. 1 and 11* (W. Strahan and T. Cadell, London, 1783).

Campbell, G., (new ed.), *The Philosophy of Rhetoric* (T. Tegg and Son, London, 1838). Originally published (1776).

Halliday, M.A.K., *Language as social semiotic: the social interpretation of language and meaning* (Edward Arnold, London, 1978).

Halliday, M.A.K., *An Introduction to Functional Grammar* (Edward Arnold, London, 1985).

Murray, Lindley, *English Grammar* (1795), Facsimile Reprint No. 106 (Menston, Scolar Press, 1968).

Contents

Introduction

There is nothing particularly original about the view that language is essentially a social phenomenon. The English philosophers Hobbes and Locke, writing in the seventeenth century, had a thoroughly social account of language in which they explained linguistic form by reference to its functions and settings in social practices. That tradition has always remained strong, if only because of its obviousness at one level. However, it is one thing to hold such a view, and quite another to attempt to construct a theory in which all aspects of linguistic activity appear as social practice, and in which all linguistic forms and processes are treated as and accounted for in terms of social forms and social processes. In part the English language itself proves to be a major obstacle to that endeavour. It is extremely difficult to write about this topic in a way that does not separate language from society as though they are discrete objects. The somewhat awkward title of this little book reflects my problems: I had tried to think of a title which did not separate 'language' from 'society' or 'culture', or language from its 'context', or talk about language and its social functions, or any of these formulations. The fact that I have not succeeded in my wish will be everywhere apparent in the book. Indeed the very structure of the English language, with its preference for nominal, object-like forms rather than for the process-oriented forms of verbs, makes it a difficult and perhaps impossible task. So, quite often where I have used ungainly and awkward circumlocutions, that has been my reason: to try and invent ways of talking in which the linguistic and the social appear as one (though this last formulation signals yet another failure!).

The tendency of English to nominalise is discussed by M.A.K. Halliday in *Spoken and Written Language* (1989).

Education is a social and cultural process like other social and cultural processes. Where it differs is in its focus, its highlighting of certain aspects of social and cultural processes. All involve the transmission of cultural values and of social meanings; though in education that is a primary focus. All social processes are in part about their own reproduction—for example, at least one function of committee meetings is to perpetuate committee meetings. Education, however, is an institution particularly focused on the reproduction of culture; that is its *raison d'être*. All social interactions involve displays of power; in education this is highlighted through a characteristic

1

conjunction of knowledge and power. But all of these features occur everywhere in all social processes and in all the texts produced on social occasions. Many other institutions are educational in this sense: the mass media, advertising, all forms of popular culture, institutionalised pleasure or leisure. All are instruments of cultural reproduction.

So although I have frequently chosen texts which come from within the social institution of education, and although I do now and again relate my argument specifically to aspects of that institution, my discussion is not one about 'language in education'. My point is rather that language in education is one instance of language in social institutions and processes. At bottom, I am interested in that interconnectedness of linguistic and social matters which has a somewhat specific form here, in education, but which is in every way recognisable from and determined by other, larger social structures. The education system, and the texts which occur in its processes, are not aberrations from the rest of social structure. That is why there is such a close homology between any particular society and its education system.

Consequently, for my examples I have chosen texts from a wide area, because I wanted to be able to compare the forms and meanings of, for instance, a casual conversation, with those of an informal interview, with those of a lesson, in order to discover both the underlying similarities and the significant differences. In that way I hope to have succeeded in showing that education is very much a part, and in no way an unusual part, of the larger social structure and of its range of texts.

My theoretical bias will be clear enough. Given the broad choice between a psychologically-based account of language and a socially-based one, my preference is for the latter. Ultimately it is, no doubt, a matter of personal preference; but well before I need to retreat to that justification I would invoke the greater explanatory power of a social theory and its greater potential usefulness. Whatever matters of a real kind that psychology might discover about language—and at the moment that is very little indeed—will turn out to be unalterably, genetically and physiologically universal, and hence (I would hope for all time) beyond change and interference. That which is not so determined is social, specific and hence at least potentially open to alteration. Within my account there is a significant place for psychology of a certain kind, concerned to provide an understanding of how the social is internalised to become the individual/psychological. Whereas psychologically-based theories place the individual (asocial) psyche at the centre, and attempt to account for the world from there, I prefer an account which places the social at the centre and attempts to account for the individual within that context.

All of this relates to my attempts to think about the question of individuality, and of the many concepts which derive from that, particularly in education, and particularly in the areas of language in education. Unlike traditional linguistic theories, including most contemporary ones, I consider the individual to have an instrumental role in the continuing process of language change, in the shaping of language. The traditional (Saussurean) view regarded the individual as

I have a preference for an account of individuality which places the social context at the centre of attention.

2

a merely passive recipient and user of the existent and established language system, which from her or his point of view was immutable. I consider the individual as social agent to be instrumentally and causally involved in the process of language change, via the constant processes of dialogue—whether in speech or in writing—aimed always at resolving differences of a larger or a smaller kind. In the course of that process, and in the construction of texts, the forms of language are constantly 'at risk', open to modification and change in the light of specific social contingencies. The individual language user is not therefore in my view impassive and impotent in the face of a monolithic language system, but is rather constantly engaged in its reconstitution and change. However, I also wished here to provide a corrective to what are in my view romantic notions of the individual, particularly as applied to children. These involve unexamined and entirely inappropriately unrealistic notions of spontaneity, creativity, and originality. Nothing at all is gained by these views, and indeed, for children much can be lost by unrealistic assumptions—literally, assumptions which have no foundation in reality. Most is gained for children by a careful analysis of what **is**, and of what, therefore, **can** be. It is here that I have attempted to provide some initial ideas.

I owe many debts. First of all to Fran Christie who asked me to write on this topic and who has been constantly helpful and patient. In writing this little book I have drawn on the ideas of many people. Among them I would like to make a particular acknowledgment to my friend and colleague, Stephen Muecke, whose ideas have influenced me much over the last few years. Everywhere here too I have continued to draw on the ideas that Bob Hodge and I developed earlier. My thinking about language continues to be shaped by the work of Michael Halliday; and it is his general conception of language activity as complex conjunctions of series of (socially/semantically) motivated choices which forms the basis of my own ideas. I owe specific debts to Arnie Goldman for allowing me to use some of his formulations on metaphor, and for being a partner in many long conversations around some of these topics. Joanne Evenden, Maree Delofski, and Debbie Lee allowed me to use materials that they had discussed in essays. John Collerson generously gave me some examples of school textbook writing, which I have used here. I owe my real initial interest in the area of language in education to Jonathan and Rachel Kress. They have been generous and forbearing suppliers of written textual materials. Grace O'Neale and Aileen Melvin cheerfully bore with my rushed manuscripts and I wish to thank them for that. Jill Brewster helped me in very many different ways, beyond the usual expression of thanks.

It is customary to absolve all those to whom thanks are due from blame for the shortcomings of the final outcome. In this case the wisdom of custom is not in any doubt for me and I happily avail myself of it.

Ferdinand de Saussure was a significant linguist in the late nineteenth and early twentieth centuries. A book based on his lectures to his students in Geneva was produced posthumously in 1915, *Course in General Linguistics*, edited by Charles Bally & Albert Sechehaye.

Chapter 1

The linguistic expression of social meaning: discourse, genre and text

The questions

In this chapter I want to focus on a set of questions central in any approach to language: How do texts arise? How do they come into being? How and why do they get produced? Why in short **do** people talk and write. In addition to saying something about the producers of texts—the speakers and writers—I also want to say something about the consumers of texts—the hearers and readers. They have tended to be regarded as pretty well passive in their relationship to texts. Some current theoretical work treats the reader/hearer's task as much more like that of the writer/speaker's, and the reading of texts is regarded as a process of the reconstruction of the text by the reader.

Other questions are associated with these. For instance, how does any one reader come to read a particular text? Do readers come across texts 'out of the blue'? Clearly the answer is 'no'. The texts that I read are in the main entirely predictable from my place in social and institutional structures. An inventory of things that I read in the course of a day would give you a pretty good indication about my social place. Similarly with my writing: a reasonably representative collection of texts written by me would give you a fairly accurate indication and description of my social place. So another set of questions to consider concerns that network of relationships in which any member of society is placed which determines the set of texts in which she or he participates as consumer and producer.

In answering these questions it is necessary to have a theory which permits a discussion in which linguistic and social matters can be addressed at all times with ease. A usual—and in my view misleading—formulation talks about moving from social to linguistic matters, or vice versa. That mode of talking presupposes a distinction between language and society as discrete objects, an effect which is further reinforced by the use of the spatial metaphor contained in 'moving from . . . to'. The three categories which I propose to use emphasise the total connectedness of linguistic and social processes, with perhaps more emphasis now on the one and now on the other. The categories are discourse, genre and text.

Linguistic and social processes are totally connected.

4

Linguistic theory has tended to approach language very much from the point of view of the speaker/writer, the producer of language; indeed linguistic theories are constructed in that way. Linguistic theories have little to say about how texts are read or heard, reconstructed and understood. Perhaps most importantly, linguistic theories are silent about the reasons for writing. Why speakers or writers should wish to speak and write, what they might want to speak and write about, and how, is not a question in linguistics. Indeed it is barely a question in communication theory, where the notions of 'transmission of information', or of 'the mutual construction/sharing of meaning' predominate.

As with most important questions, the obviousness of the matter has precluded its being perceived as a problem. However, we can quickly focus the significance of that question if we see it in a cross-cultural context. We know that speakers from other cultures do not talk about issues in the way we do, we know that issues in our culture are not issues in other cultures, in short, that ways of talking as well as the topics of our talk are entirely cultural constructs. Given the total interconnection, the unity of linguistic and of cultural questions, it is a matter that has to be taken up in any theory of language.

In an area such as education, these questions have to be central. On the one hand, the very processes of education are linguistically constituted—the interactions of teacher and students, student and student, parent and child, parent and school, school and community—are all formed and expressed in verbal texts. To understand the processes it is essential to understand how these texts come into being, how they are constituted, how they are reproduced in reading or hearing, and assimilated, why certain texts become generated, and why others are impossible. On the other hand, every aspect of education is about transmission of a society's culture in its verbal form so that a thorough understanding of texts, their constitution, construction and effects is entirely essential.

Institutions, meanings and discourses

The starting point of my account is the listener/reader, speaker/writer, seen **not** as an isolated individual, but as a social agent, located in a network of social relations, in specific places in a social structure.

For that social agent the grammar of a language, its syntax, phonology, and lexicon, has a very specific look, not 'language as such' but rather a particular set of potentials and possibilities within the whole language system. For her or him certain facets of the linguistic system are familiar, accessible, in constant use. Others will seem strange, used by speakers beyond the social grouping of this language user, in different work or professional environments, by members of other social classes or ethnic groupings, or maybe differentiated by age or gender. This is not more than our commonsense observation that not everyone who speaks, say English, speaks or writes it as we do. We may understand the other's use of English and yet find it quite difficult—more or less—and in some cases incomprehensible. Even where we find the

The individual must be understood primarily as a social agent, located in a network of social relations.

other's language quite comprehensible, it may be that we would not in any situation use that language ourselves.

How is this phenomenon to be explained? It is part of all our experience. The manager may be as conscious of her or his distinctly different language use as the worker on the shopfloor is, and unable to use the worker's language. The professional may be awkward about her or his use of language to a client, and as awkward in using the client's language as the client is in attempting to use the professional's. As it is part of all of our experience, it has been the subject of theorising in linguistics. Notions such as speech community, speech event, and code switching point to important elements and give necessary insights. They are however, explanations from the standpoint of linguistics alone. The notion of speech community is, as its label declares, a linguistically-motivated term. It describes a particular type of phenomenon, but gives no explanation why there is this community, that is, why a group of people do happen to use, in a particular place and situation and at a given time, a form of language similar enough for a linguist to recognise a speech community.

An explanation for differing modes and forms of speaking can only be given when we look at the phenomenon from a linguistic **and** social perspective. Then we find that these speakers share membership in a particular social institution, with its practices, its values, its meanings, its demands, prohibitions, and permissions. We also begin to get an explanation for the **kind** of language that is being used, that is the kinds of texts that have currency and prominence in that community, and the forms, contents and functions of those texts.

Take 'education' as an example of such an institution. A sociolinguist might well have discovered that educators form a 'speech community'. They use forms of language, at least in certain places and at certain times, which share noticeable similarities: words, expressions, 'ways of saying things'; that is, a grammar which is characteristic of that group; texts which occur nowhere else, such as tests, essays, examinations, lessons, staff-room conversations, and so on. But to get an explanation for one or all of them, one has to attend to education not as a LINGUISTIC but as a SOCIAL institution; preferably, to see it as an institution whose social meanings are linguistically expressed, linguistically reinforced through constant use of its language, and constantly recreated/reproduced through the use of forms of language which in all its aspects carries and expresses the meanings of that institution.

Educators know how pervasive the hold is that the institution has on them through its modes of action, linguistic action foremost among these. The modes of talking tend to pervade other areas of life, not necessarily connected with that institution. Teachers can come to see the whole world as a classroom, and in their everyday lives treat every interaction as a lesson. In that they do not differ from any other group whose institution has clearly articulated behaviours, values and forms of language—doctors, policemen and women, and lawyers, for example.

Institutions and social groupings have specific meanings and values which are articulated in language in **systematic ways**. Following the work particularly of the French philosopher Michel Foucault, I refer to these systematically-organised modes of talking as DISCOURSE.

The terms 'speech community', 'speech event' and 'code switching' have all been variously associated with different traditions of sociolinguistic research.

Education is a social institution whose meanings are linguistically expressed.

6

Discourses are systematically-organised sets of statements which give expression to the meanings and values of an institution. Beyond that, they define, describe and delimit what it is possible to say and not possible to say (and by extension—what it is possible to do or not to do) with respect to the area of concern of that institution, whether marginally or centrally. A discourse provides a set of possible statements about a given area, and organises and gives structure to the manner in which a particular topic, object, process is to be talked about. In that it provides descriptions, rules, permissions and prohibitions of social and individual actions.

Discourses tend towards exhaustiveness and inclusiveness; that is, they attempt to account not only for an area of immediate concern to an institution, but attempt to account for increasingly wider areas of concern. Take as an example one discourse which determines the manner in which the biological category of sex is taken into social life as gender, the discourse of sexism. It specifies what men and women may be, how they are to think of themselves, how they are to think of and to interrelate with the other gender. But beyond that the discourse of sexism specifies what families may be, and relations within the family: what it is to be a 'proper father' or 'a mother', the 'eldest son', 'our little girl'. It reaches into all major areas of social life, specifying what work is suitable, possible even, for men and for women; how pleasure is to be seen by either gender; what artistic possibilities if any there are for either gender. A metaphor which I use to explain the effects of discourse to myself is that of a military power whose response to border skirmishes is to occupy the adjacent territory. As problems continue, more territory is occupied, then settled and colonised. A discourse colonises the social world imperialistically, from the point of view of one institution.

Other examples come readily to mind: religious discourse, nationalistic discourse (what it is to be 'a good Australian') and so on. Returning for a moment to the discourse of the institution of education: it is not that long ago that this determined what teachers or students at teachers' colleges could or could not do even in their 'private' lives, regulated the interrelationships of gender through segregation in schools (interacting here with sexist discourse), and placed injunctions on sexual relations, and marriage, for mature members of the education profession. To the extent that this is no longer the case, the domain of educational discourse has both contracted and altered.

Discourses do not exist in isolation but within a larger system of sometimes opposing, contradictory, contending, or merely different discourses. Given that each discourse tends towards the colonisation of larger areas, there are dynamic relations between these which ensure continuous shifts and movement, progression or withdrawal in certain areas.

To exemplify some of the points I have been making, here are three short extracts from larger texts. In reading each extract, attempt to bear in mind these questions:

1 Why is this topic being written about?
2 How is the topic being written about?
3 What other ways of writing about the topic are there?

The first extract is from *Cleo*, June 1984.

Miss Mouse
This type is a dead give-away. The first thing you notice is her posture—rounded shoulders, hands in lap, head cast down and she's fidgeting, always fidgeting. She would never initiate a conversation and if asked a question, she's likely to whisper a non-committal response or just shrug her shoulders and smile wanly. Her clothes are neat, but she doesn't have much sense of style: conservative, safe skirt and blouse, usually in bland colours, very few accessories (if anything, a single watch band) and her hair is usually silky clean and caught up with a head band.

Miss Mouse should try always to sit up straight (even if it is a strain) and find a magazine to read in waiting situations (thus fidgeting would be unnecessary). Clothes: check out magazine fashion pages for some ideas on how to inject touches of colour to an outfit without compromising style, and consider a brighter lipstick to liven up your face.

(*Cleo*, June 1984)

My answer to the first question is 'to instruct women about how to see themselves, and to tell both men and women what type of women to value'. The question arises in sexist discourse, and, to answer my second question, is written about in sexist discourse. Other ways of writing about this topic are provided through the extensive analyses, particularly by feminist writers, of sexist discourse. To make my point that this text is constructed in sexist discourse whose operations are general in our society, here is an extract from a Mills and Boon romance, *No Quiet Refuge*.

No quiet refuge
Five years ago when they had both been seventeen, Hilary had kicked her school hat into a hedge on their last day at school, and declared:

'That's school, that's Ravensmere. Coming to London with me, Mercy?'

It had been a terrific idea, Mercy had thought then. But her father had soon put a stop to that. 'You're going to secretarial college, young lady,' he had told her forcefully. 'Jack Driver can let his daughter do what he likes—but you're staying home.'

And she had stayed home. And for a whole year she had pined for the fabulous time Hilary wrote she was having. As Hilary had said, 'Nothing ever happens in Ravensmere.'

After her secretarial training Mercy had started work at the local school. Then, suddenly, she wasn't longing to join Hilary any more. For Philip, a teacher at the same school, had begun asking her out. She had known him to say 'Hello' to for years, but gradually, the more she got to know him, the more she began to value his worth.

They had started to date regularly, though at first she had been fearful her father might not like him. But her father too had seen that Philip was the right man for her. It was a joy to her that he had raised no objection to their becoming engaged.

Shortly after their engagement nearly a year ago, her father had acted upon what he had been talking of for years, telling her mother that with Mercy more or less settled, he was going to sell the house and that the two of them were going to Australia to live.

Philip had been a darling in those early days when she missed her mother acutely. And if there was a fly in Mercy's particular jar of ointment in that Philip had a mother too, a mother who must have off-loaded her share of human charity on to her son, for she had none, then Mercy tried hard to be as generous as Philip in his views of other people. She had never heard him say an unkind word about anyone.

Perhaps that was why it had come as something of a shock, when she told him Hilary had invited her to be her bridesmaid, to hear him ask:

'What does she want you for?'

Taken aback because he had never shown any of the aggression that was part and parcel of her father, she'd had to think for a moment, why indeed should the sophisticated Hilary want her for a bridesmaid.

'I'm—her friend,' she had brought out at last.

'But you haven't seen her for years.'

That was true enough. Hilary's last visit to Ravensmere had been a flying one, no time to look up old friends.

'That doesn't mean we're not friends still. We correspond . . .'

'Spasmodically,' Philip had put in, and she had been aghast that she and Philip, who never quarrelled, should suddenly appear to be in the middle of an argument.

'W—would you rather I didn't accept?' she questioned, quieting something in her that was objecting to her being so amenable.

But she was glad she had offered, even if she wasn't very sure about her offer. For Philip was suddenly her Philip again.

'Of course you must be her bridesmaid. Of course you must.' He squeezed her hand, and Mercy felt good again. Philip appeared to think Hilary was not quite the right sort of friend for her. But, as she had known, he was too generous, too kind and gentle to want to spoil things for her.

Though, strangely, she was troubled again to find later, after she had said goodnight to him, that a flicker of rebellion should make itself felt when she recalled his question of whether Hilary would be paying for her . . .

(Jessica Steele, *No Quiet Refuge*, Mills & Boon, London, n.d., pp. 6–7)

Mercy, the character in this romance, is an improved Miss Mouse, constructed with an admixture of the liberated female, but her kinship to Miss Mouse is not too difficult to see. The third extract comes from a high-school textbook. Again, try to bear in mind my three questions.

Squandering our inheritance

We would have little respect for a young man who inherited great wealth but spent it so quickly that he died in poverty and left nothing to his heirs. But that is exactly the sort of thing the human race as a whole is doing today. We have inherited the earth and all it contains but we are using up its resources at a rate which, already alarming, is increasing rapidly. Unless drastic changes are made soon, our descendants will inherit a much poorer world.

How has this situation come about? First, the unprecedented rise in population (see Chapter 12) has meant greatly increased pressure on the world's resources. Second, the revolution in science and technology which has been mainly responsible for the accelerated population growth has raised living standards to new levels in the developed nations. People in these countries not only expect high standards of living but hope for continued improvement. People in the underdeveloped nations are naturally anxious to be able to reach similar standards. Governments and economists throughout the world have been obsessed with the idea of constant growth. The result has been an enormously increased demand for food, raw materials and energy. A contributing factor has been the extremely wasteful nature of large-scale commercial enterprise concerned only with increased sales (see Figure 14.4).

Part of the mischief has resulted from the belief that the resources of the world are inexhaustible or that even if we run out of some vital commodity, scientists will be able to find a satisfactory substitute. Such ideas are very dangerous, as they lull people into a sense of false security while irreparable damage is being done.

(*Survival: Man and his World Book 4*, Macmillan, Melbourne, 1975, p. 199)

Several discourses are at work here, as the answers to my questions would reveal: a moralistic/conservationist discourse determines why this topic is chosen; and it is written about in terms largely of that discourse. There are traces of sexist discourse, in the metaphor which sets the tone for the discussion. Other modes of talking about the topic of natural resources are obviously available, and the text would be entirely different written from the point of view of a capitalist/economic discourse.

In the colonisation of areas of social life, discourses attempt to reconcile contradictions, mismatches, disjunctions and discontinuities within that domain by making that which is social seem natural and that which is problematic seem obvious.

The effect is that the areas accounted for within one discourse offer no spaces for analysis, everything is of one piece, a seamless fabric of tightly interwoven strands. The accounts provided within one discourse become not only unchallenged, but unchallengeable, as 'common sense'. If the domination of a particular area by a discourse is successful it provides an integrated and plausible account of that area, which allows no room for thought; the social will have been turned into the natural. At that stage it is impossible to conceive of alternative modes of thought, or else alternative modes of thought will seem bizarre, outlandish, unnatural.

Given this view of language (itself the product of the interplay of discourses) it can be seen how the speaking/writing and reading/ listening of individuals is determined by their positions in institutions, by their place within certain discourses and by their place particularly in intersecting sets of discourses. It allows us to link speaking and writing, listening and reading to social place and to social/institutional meanings, without giving up a serious notion of the individual as social agent.

Texts and the motivations of texts

Discourses strive towards total and encompassing accounts in which contradictions are resolved or at least suppressed. If problematic areas are resolved in this way, and the social is made natural, when everything is both 'obviously natural' and 'naturally obvious', what then is there to talk about? What is the motivation for speech? There are two answers of a broadly similar kind. Within any social group there are a number of discourses, because a number of significant institutions operate within any one social group. Hence any group will be using a number of discourses offering alternative or contradictory accounts of reality. That is, even though any one discourse accounts for the area of its relevance, there are overlapping areas of interest where differing accounts are offered, which are contested by several discourses. Take a capitalist economic discourse on the one hand and a Christian religious one on the other. The one suggests that the 'natural' condition of 'man' is to be acquisitive, competitive and aggressive, and that society is founded on a dynamic where individuals acquire power by depriving others of their power. The other enjoins its adherents to divest themselves of wealth, to be meek, to offer the other cheek.

In western technological societies, capitalist economic discourses have co-existed for several centuries with Christian religious ones. Countless sermons have been preached in a constant attempt at an ideological reconciliation of these two discourses. More recently these two discourses have entered a new and antagonistic relationship, with the growth of liberation theology.

For any member of a social group discursive multiplicity, contestation, and difference is both a description of their history and an account of their present social position at any given moment. The individual's history is composed of the experience of a range of discourses, passing through the intimate relations of the family and its discourses of authority, gender, morality, religion, politics; into school and its discourses of knowledge, science, authority, aesthetics; to work and adulthood. The discursive history of each individual therefore bears the traces of the discourses associated with the social places which that indivudal has occupied and experienced. These form, like sedimentary layers, the linguistic experience and potential of the speaker. It can be seen how individuals from similar social positions, with similar social histories, have significantly similar linguistic experiences and therefore have quite similar forms of language available to them. At the same time, to the extent that the discursive histories of individuals differ—a situation more likely than that of total congruence for many members of social groups—their experience of language, their positioning towards the linguistic system, differ. Added to this is the present social position of an individual: depending on their place in social institutions—work/profession, leisure, family, political affiliations, sexual relations—their present experience of discourses will differ.

> Individuals from similar social positions have similar linguistic experiences, and therefore similar forms of language available to them.

A theory of language based on this account explains two fundamental factors at one and the same time: the social determination of an individual's knowledge of language on the one hand, and individual difference and differing position *vis-à-vis* the linguistic system on the other. A theory which makes no allowance for the social determination of linguistic practice is obviously deficient; at the same time a theory which ignores individual difference in linguistic practice—a matter equally apparent to any observer—is also deficient. In a discourse-oriented theory of language both find a plausible and motivated account. This account leaves aside factors whose importance is difficult to assess, namely those differences which may be due to biological variation and to intangibles such as the concept of imagination.

Difference and texts

The social/discursive histories of individuals, as well as their present social position, determine their access to the set of discourses in a society. The unresolved tensions among the discourses used by the one speaker, and those used in interaction, produce a need for discursive resolution. There are likely to be problems at any time, arising out of unresolved differences in the individual's discursive history, the individual's present discursive location and the context of discourses in interactions. That difference is the motor that produces texts. Every text arises out of a particular problematic. Texts are therefore manifestations of discourses and the meanings of discourses, and the sites of attempts to resolve particular problems.

Texts are (1) manifestations of discourse; (2) the meanings of discourses; and (3) the sites of attempts to resolve problems.

Dialogues, whether conversations, interviews, or debates, are the clearest examples. In their structure they display discursive difference at every point. Where there is no difference, no text comes into being. The playwright Harold Pinter has explored situations of this kind in a number of plays. Here is an extract from the opening of *The Birthday Party*:

Act One

	Meg	Is that you, Petey?
	Pause	
		Petey, is that you?
	Pause	
5		Petey?
	Petey	What?
	Meg	Is that you?
	Petey	Yes, it's me.
	Meg	What? Are you back?
10	Petey	Yes.
	Meg	I've got your cornflakes ready. Here's your cornflakes. Are they nice?
	Petey	Very nice.
	Meg	I thought they'd be nice. You got your paper?
15	Petey	Yes.
	Meg	Is it good?
	Petey	Not bad.
	Meg	What does it say?
	Petey	Nothing much.

20	Meg	You read me out some nice bits yesterday.
	Petey	Yes, well, I haven't finished this one yet.
	Meg	Will you tell me when you come to something good?
	Petey	Yes.
	Pause	
25	Meg	Have you been working hard this morning?
	Petey	No. Just stacked a few of the old chairs. Cleaned up a bit.
	Meg	Is it nice out?

[stage directions deleted]   (H. Pinter, *The Birthday Party*, Methuen, London, 1960)

There is no discursive difference here; the long war of attrition of matrimony has eliminated such differences as existed for this couple. Meg nevertheless wishes to avoid silence and attempts to construct difference, while Petey refuses to acknowledge her attempt. Hence the dynamic of this interaction is one of an attempt to construct difference, followed by a refusal to acknowledge that difference (as a sufficiently substantial difference), an abandonment of that segment of the interaction, a renewed attempt to construct difference, and so on. It is not a successful conversation; the only difference that motivates it is Meg's wish to have some interaction, which forces Petey into the minimal response of a refusal. Successful dialogues come about in the tension between (discursive) difference and the attempt to resolve that difference in some way.

As an example of a dialogue where difference exists and provides the dynamic of the text, consider this extract from an interview between a sociologist and a 'middle manager'. The middle manager had been to a training course designed to induct him into middle-management; the sociologist was interested to know how the training course imbued the participants with the ideology of middle-management.

Interview

	Frank	Yeah, informal contact with staff members, was that useful?
	Ted	Staff members, in which sense?
	Frank	The people who were running the Course.
	Ted	No, I don't think so. Well useful, it was very profitable.
5	Frank	Why, they bought all the drinks? [laugh]
	Ted	No, with one of the staff members I played cards until three o'clock one morning and took about seven quid off him, but apart from that . . . If they will play cards, that's you know, one has to pay for one's learning, and we had a little sort of teach-
10		in on how not to gamble.
	Frank	Do you think of yourself as a Manager?
	Ted	[long pause—11 seconds] No, I think of myself as part of management. I think there's a difference.
		[3 second pause] The difference is maybe only apparent to
15		someone that exists inside this particular organisation, but I manage very few people. I'm more of a resource, really, to the people who do manage.
	Frank	Who are they? Where would you locate them?
	Ted	All through the factory, [Frank: Hm, hm] at every level, not only

20   to the people that manage, they're resource to everyone, if they
      happen to manage [Frank: Yeah] okay, but people would consult
      me on matters appertaining to management. If you take, it's
      always been my [3 second pause] uh my sort of,
      um, theory that if you [pause] take [pause] the, um sort of us
25   and them philosophy, the only them that the majority of people
      inside the factory can identify tends to be the personnel
      department, because it's the them that say you know and how
      your holidays sort out, it's them that says why their pay was held
      up, so you know the faceless them is perhaps
30   represented by the personnel department, and if us and them
      is management and worker, then I suppose we're part of the
      management set-up.

Difference is apparent, at every level. On the surface it concerns the definition of the term 'manager'; beneath the surface it is difference about the purposes of the two participants—a barely concealed hostility on the part of the interviewee and an insistence on achieving his aims on the part of the interviewer. Once the interviewee acquiesces in his role, the text revolves around the difference between contrasting discourses on management. Here that is a difference between a conception of management as a hierarchically-organised power structure on the one hand (where there are 'managers'), and a conception of management as 'teamwork' on the other, (where an employee thinks of himself as 'part of management'). In the 'manager-discourse', power is located in individuals. Grammatically this is manifested, for instance, in the use of the human/animate pronoun *who* (*to the people who do manage*). In the 'management-discourse' power resides in the group, conceived of not in terms of a collection of individuals but in terms of a commodity, a *resource* (*I'm more of a resource, really*). The pronoun which characterises this discourse is the non-human/inanimate *that* (*someone that exists inside this particular organisation, it's them that says. . .*). The verb *exists*—rather than *works*, or *is employed*—is revealing in that respect.

While interviews display the structure of difference particularly clearly, all texts are constructed around this dynamic. Even texts constructed by one speaker or writer are no exception. Take the sentence I have just written, and you have just read: 'Even texts constructed by one speaker or writer are no exception'. It was motivated by a silent dialogue of myself with an imagined other interactant to whom I had attributed a view something like: 'Yes, but what about single speaker texts? Surely **they're** not about difference; they're just someone telling you something, just giving you some information.' My 'Even texts. . .' was a response to that imagined view. The last 19 lines of the interview above are a clear example of the different voices which contend around the meaning of 'management' and give rise to this section of the larger text.

Dialogue is for that reason the linguistic mode which is fundamental to an understanding of language and its uses. In dialogue the constitution of texts in and around difference is most readily apparent. Here it can be most readily discovered, analysed and described, and the processes of resolution of differences traced to their more or less satisfactory conclusions. Most speech genres are ostensibly about difference: argument (differences of an ideological kind), interview (differences around power and knowledge), 'gossip' (difference around informal knowledge), lecture (difference around formal knowledge), conversation. But as I pointed out above, single speaker and writer texts are no less constituted in difference and constructed around its resolution than are dialogues. Indeed the task of the author/writer is precisely this: to attempt to construct a text in which discrepancies, contradictions, and disjunctions are bridged, covered over, eliminated.

All texts are constituted in difference.

A particularly charged example is that of a political leader. The discursive task of the leader is constant; the detail of its execution differs, depending on the group of which she or he is leader. Where the group is well established, the leader's task is to produce texts which function as paradigm examples of the relevant discourse(s) and function continuously to reproduce and reconstitute the group around the discourse(s). The task of the leader may also be one of recruiting new members, as in the speeches and manifestos of political leaders at election time. Here individuals with discursive allegiances other than those of the leader's group have to be addressed via a text which offers them the possibility of affiliation. Lastly, the leader's task may be to give definition and coherence to an entirely new group. In such a case it is the leader's task to construct texts which offer the possibility of assimilation of hitherto disparate discourses and to hold out the promise of unification, coherence and plausibility of a new grouping constituted initially entirely by the manner in which discourses are brought together in texts. The formation of a new political party would be a good example. Note that this procedure reverses the usual social/linguistic process where discourses arise out of social institutions and give rise to specific texts. In this case there is no such institution; if the leader is successful, an institution may be formed through the operation of texts.

Take as an example the anti-nuclear movement. A very disparate set of groups come together under this broad banner. In Australia (unlike in the United Kingdom for instance) it includes groups opposed to the mining of uranium, concerned with the issue of land rights, groups opposed to the continued existence of US bases and facilities, groups opposed to nuclear weapons on various grounds, and many others. No single institutional basis unites them. Any text constructed to address that large group faces the problem of bringing together discourses of a most disparate kind, and attempting to construct a text in which these are brought together in a coherent, plausible manner. It is a daunting task, perhaps an impossible one. Here are some brief extracts from a speech given by Dr Helen Caldicott at the Palm Sunday Peace March on Sunday, 15 April 1984, in Sydney.

Speech

Thank you, thank you fellow Australians. You're a great country. [loud clapping and shouts] This is the best country in the world. [clapping] And that's why we have an enormous responsibility because we have to lead the earth to survival, and it's Australia that started it fourteen years ago with the

French tests. It was us who took the lead to take the French to the Court of Justice at The Hague, to discipline her. And now she tests underground, and it was marches like this that stopped the French blowing up bombs in the Pacific. When I tell the Americans what the Australians did about the French tests they all stand up and cheer. The Americans think that the Australians are fantastic people. [clapping, yells] Then Australia took the stand against uranium mining.

. . . They haven't seen the last epidemic. How many leaders of the world, and mostly the leaders of the world are old men . . . that's true isn't it? . . . Reagan and Cherenkov are old men . . . how many leaders of the world have watched the explosion of a single hydrogen bomb . . . felt the heat on their face two hundred miles away . . . like an oven door opening . . . watched the bomb explode through their hands and their closed eyes and the bones of their hand light up . . . seen a battleship rise up in the water like a splinter and disappear? How many leaders of the world have helped a child to die? . . . of leukemia . . . and supported the parents before and forever after in their grief. You've all lost somebody you loved: a parent, a child, a relative or a friend. You know the grief it leaves and you never get over it. I suggest that the people of . . . who are running the world, if they're not in touch with their feelings, they're not appropriate people to be running the world in this nuclear age . . . and we should get rid of them.

. . . bomb's gonna come in, it's gonna come in at twenty times the speed of sound at tree top level and explode right here on us in the fraction of a millionth of a second with the heat of the sun . . . and it will dig a hole right here three quarters of a mile wide and eight hundred feet deep. And of all of us, and all of these buildings and all of the earth below will just go up in the mushroom cloud as radioactive molecules up there into the stratosphere. Six miles from . . .

. . . is our planet. We are brothers and sisters with the Chinese and with the Russians and with the Americans, we are one human race, one humanity. [applause] One humanity, one spirit, one earth. And it's interesting, and one death . . . that's right, we'll all go together when we go. And it's interesting that great psychiatrist Jesus who lived two thousand years ago said it's easy to love your friend, what it's hard to do is love your enemy, and the nuclear age has brought us full circle now to know that we have to actually love those Russians, because it's not up to us or Bob Hawke or Ronald Reagan whether or not we live or die, it's up to the Russians . . . And they're paranoid, that's why they shot down that jet. When a paranoid patient comes into hospital you don't threaten them you . . .

. . . playing yet'. A little boy aged eight stood up before some doctors and said, 'nobody wants to be given a broken present at Christmas, that's how I feel about my life'. What have we done to our children? And there aren't communist babies or capitalist babies. A baby is a baby is a baby. [applause, sedate] And next time you see a baby, a tiny new-born baby, look into its eyes and see the incredible innocence in those eyes and the archetypal wisdom, and know it's the babies we're going to save. The babies and the planet now and forever more. We have to give up as it says . . .

. . . of time. Will man evolve spiritually and emotionally enough . . . and women, to know that we can't fight and we have to live together in peace. If we can't we'll blow up the world and you and I will know that in our lifetime.

Before we die, we will know whether the human race can do it or not. If we die in a nuclear holocaust, we'll know we failed. If we die of natural causes in our lifetime, we'll definitely know that we succeeded. You can do nothing less with your life than this . . . to give up everything for the planet. And even if you fail, as the bomb goes off, you can die with a clear conscience. But it makes the earth so precious and I really and truly believe that the people of the earth are rising up and the politicians will have to stand aside and give us what we want. We want the earth to continue and we want to live; and have children and life to go on for evermore. [applause]

A number of quite distinct discourses operate here: medical, Christian, populist, (Jungian) psychiatric, patriotic, sentimental/parental, romantic, patriarchal, technological, prophetic, feminist. The traces of these different discourses are evident enough; they have not been closely integrated by the writer/speaker into anything like a seamless text: the discursive differences are not resolved. Consequently the text is unlikely to provide that definitional impulse which would act to give unity to the diverse groups which had assembled on that day to hear this speech. Although the text is that of a single writer the contention of the different discourses is clearly evident, so much so in fact that it has been beyond the writer's ability to control that difference. It would not be difficult to imagine this text as a dialogue among a number of speakers: the 'parts' would not be hard to assign. It would be a somewhat static dialogue, a bit like an initial declaration of position, but a dialogue nonetheless.

The underlying dialogic nature of this text gives rise to the question about the function of author/writers generally. I mentioned above that in this instance it is to control and if possible to eliminate difference, perhaps to establish the dominance of one discourse. If that is not possible the author/writer might attempt to use the text to alter the manner in which particular readers will read and reconstruct this and other texts. If it is the case that we read certain texts because of where we are situated socially/institutionally, and if it is also the case that we read these texts in certain ways, determined by our social place and our discursive history, then a particular text might be used to alter the way in which we read all texts. If our readings are determined by a particular position which we 'have' or adopt, it might be possible to construct a new coherent reading position for future texts. Tony Bennett, in *Texts in history: The determinations of readings and their texts*, uses the term 'reading formation' to talk about the

set of discursive and inter-textual determination which organise and animate the practice of reading, connecting texts and readers in specific relations to one another in constituting readers as reading subjects of particular types and texts as objects-to-be-read in particular ways. This entails arguing that texts have and can have no existence independently of such reading formations, that there is no place independent of, anterior to or above the varying reading formations through which historical life is variantly modulated within which texts can be constituted as objects of knowledge.

(T. Bennett, 'Texts in history: The determinations of readings and their texts' in P. Widdowson (ed.), *Re-reading English*, Methuen, London, 1982)

The function of the writer is to construct texts which confirm or alter the manner in which particular texts are read.

Educational texts and difference

The institution of education is constituted around difference, a difference of knowledge, power, age, and frequently one of class. All the texts which are produced within the education system therefore are motivated by difference. However, if this is true of all texts, how does this characteristic differentiate the texts of education from any other text? The answer is that difference as such does not distinguish one set of texts from another: what does distinguish them are the areas of difference. A question such as, 'What kinds of discourses are in contention here?' will prove to be revealing. In relation to texts from educational institutions it is important to understand what discourses of knowledge, of morals, of authority, of gender, of power, appear and which of these are dominant in constituting the texts. This can give a revealing insight into the real contents—the hidden curricula—of any occasion within the larger scale processes of education.

The concept of difference does however have a particular significance in the context of education. Success in education, for both teacher and learner, is defined by the extent to which difference is overcome. A knowledge of the nature of the difference and of the strategies of resolution of difference are therefore crucial for both teacher and learner. From the child's point of view success depends first of all on understanding how the difference is constituted and accepting the manner of its constitution, and secondly on understanding and accepting the modes of its resolution. A rejection of one or both inevitably leads to distancing, alienation and failure.

A teacher's function is to construct particular kinds of readers.

The teacher's function—and that of the education system at large—is like that of the political leader/writer, that is, to construct her or his students as particular kinds of readers, to construct for them reading positions *vis-à-vis* a very large set of texts, those of the culture as a whole.

Kinds of texts: genre

Language always happens as text, and not as isolated words and sentences. From an aesthetic, social or educational perspective it is the text which is the significant unit of language. Texts arise in specific social situations and they are constructed with specific purposes by one or more speakers or writers. Meanings find their expression in text—though the origins of meanings are outside the text—and are negotiated (about) in texts, in concrete situations of social exchange. Texts are the material form of language; in particular, texts give material realisation to discourses. Hence the meanings of texts are in part the meanings of the discourses which are present in and have given rise to a specific text.

18

The social occasions of which texts are a part have a fundamentally important effect on texts. The characteristic features and structures
of those situations, the purposes of the participants, the goals of the
participants all have their effects on the form of the texts which are
constructed in those situations. The situations are always conventional.
That is, the occasions on which we interact, the social relations which
we contract, are conventionalised and structured, more or less
thoroughly, depending on the kind of situation it is. They range from
entirely formulaic and ritualised occasions, such as royal weddings,
sporting encounters, committee meetings, to family rituals such as
breakfast or barbecues or fights over who is to do the dishes. Other,
probably fewer occasions are less ritualised, less formulaic; casual conversations may be an example. The structures and forms of the conventionalised occasions themselves signify the functions, the purposes
of the participants, and the desired goals of that occasion.

Take, as an example, a committee meeting. It is an occasion which
is highly conventional and ritualised; its conventions and rituals have
specific functions and goals. These might be characterised broadly as
the intention to reach decisions in certain ways, to involve designated
categories of people in decision making, and to reach decisions which
are seen as equitable and politically sustainable. These functions and
goals, conventions and rituals, have effects on the texts which arise
on such occasions, and give rise to conventionalised forms of texts which
are themselves expressions of the meanings of the social occasions on
which they arose.

The conventionalised forms of the occasions lead to conventionalised forms of texts, to specific GENRES. Genres have specific forms
and meanings, deriving from and encoding the functions, purposes and
meanings of the social occasions. Genres therefore provide a precise
index and catalogue of the relevant social occasions of a community
at a given time. A few examples of genre are : interview, essay, conversation, sale, tutorial, sports commentary, seduction, office memo, novel,
political speech, editorial, sermon, joke, instruction.

The term 'genre' is
used extensively
in *Language
Education* (Christie
1989), *Language and
Gender* (Poynton
1989), and *Factual
Writing* (Martin
1989).

Some genres have received a significant amount of detailed study.
Traditionally only literary genres had been the subject of attention, so
that we know quite a lot about the forms of sonnets, short stories,
novellas, epics, and so on. Literary scholars did not generally make
a connection between literary genres and social occasions—though it
is not difficult to do so. Outside literature, genres that have received
particular attention over the last decade or so have been interviews and
classroom lessons. Interviews and lessons share certain features : their
conventional and ritualised form is readily discernible and describable;
they are genres in which texts are constructed by more than one participant, one of whom has significantly greater power assigned by the
genre—the interviewer and the teacher; the more powerful participant
controls and shapes the text. One well-known example of the study of
a classroom talk is that of John Sinclair and Malcom Coulthard,
Towards an Analysis of Discourse.

See Sinclair &
Coulthard (1975).

Sinclair and Coulthard did not make a connection between the
forms of this genre, and the functions and meanings of the social
occasion, that is, of the lesson, of the curriculum, and of the education

See Fowler, Hodge,
Kress & Trew
(1979).

The meanings of text
derive both from the
discourse and the
genre of which the
text is representative.

system more generally. Their analysis is detailed enough and of a kind to allow such a connection to be established without great difficulty. Examples of the analysis of interviews may be found in Fowler et al. (1979) in the chapters 'Interviews' and 'The ideology of middle-management'. In these descriptions there is an attempt to relate the formal (linguistic) features of the interviews to the functions and meanings of the social situation, and the purposes of the participants.

The meanings of texts are therefore derived not only from the meanings of the discourse which give rise to and appear in particular texts, but also from the meanings of the genre of a particular text. Both discourse and genre carry specific and socially determined meanings. Discourse carries meanings about the nature of the institution from which it derives; genre carries meanings about the conventional social occasions on which texts arise.

Texts are therefore doubly determined: by the meanings of the discourses which appear in the text, and by the forms, meanings and constraints of a particular genre. Both discourse and genre arise out of the structures and processes of a society: discourses are derived from the larger social institutions within a society; genres are derived from the conventionalised social occasions on and through which social life is carried on. Clearly, these two kinds of meanings are not at all unrelated and consequently there can be matching and overlappings between certain discourses and certain genres. There are preferred conjunctions of discourses and genres, and prohibitions on other conjunctions. For example, the social institution of medicine has given rise to medical discourse. That institution (or sub-groupings of it) also has conventionalised occasions, such as lectures, (the writing of) scientific papers, meetings, research committees, experimentation, job interviews, conversations, formal dinner speeches, etc. Because there is a close link between the nature of the institution and the kinds of occasions that characterise it, at times it seems as though discourse and genre are identical. However that is not so. It is easy to demonstrate that many of the occasions (and genres) of the institution of medicine occur in many quite separate institutions while the generic features remain constant.

To make my discussion somewhat more concrete I will discuss a number of texts, or parts of texts. First I will look at part of a conversation and compare that with an interview. I will then compare both with an example of the genre of lesson, and conclude with a brief discussion of another educational genre, the textbook. None of my analyses will be very detailed and certainly not definitive. My intention is to draw out some characteristic features, show how they interrelate with the social occasion, and highlight the importance of genre.

A conversation

Max   A time perhaps before writing was invented when the ability to handle language in a public way in a formal way in a public way certainly in a ritualised way would have been **prized** that is that ah that early classical oratory even even when there was a written
5   language that the written language wasn't prized as highly as the as the spoken language.

Jim   Well amm I'll . . . one of the factors involved in the difference

20

between speech and writing and um and ah ah private and public
is of course formality and of course it also goes back to
10   the notion of mass communication.

  Max   Hm

  Jim   When . . . that is if your audience is a mass audience ahm then
the level of interaction with the audience is likely to be more
formal so if you have ah ah ah a social group ah for whom ah
15   language exists only in the single medium of ah speech then
you'll have ah different forms of speech varying ah in degree of
formality.

  Max   a Hm a Hm

  Jim   Ahm and that degree of formality depends on the relations with
20   the audience. . .

  Max   Because you can get to a larger audience. . ..

As this is a genre within the spoken mode of language, certain features of conversation have to do with the nature and structure of speech. So for instance the syntax is that of clause-chains, rather than that of sentences, that is clauses tend to be adjoined, co-ordinated, conjoined in a sequence rather than being subordinated, embedded, integrated in the hierarchical structure of sentences. A typical example is *When . . . that is if your audience is a mass audience ahm then the level of interaction with the audience is likely to be more formal so if you have ah ah ah a social group ah for whom ah language exists only in the single medium of ah speech then you'll have . . .* (lines 12−16). There are hesitations, which indicate that the speaker is 'thinking on the spot', and doing so in a situation which is informal enough to permit this without the penalty of being thought and classified as 'inarticulate'. Turns are taken on the initiative of the one who wishes to speak, and are taken by establishing overt cohesive links with the text of the preceding speaker. For instance, lines 7−8 *difference between speech and writing . . .* takes up lines 5−6 . . . *written language . . . spoken language . . ..* That is, usually the overt formal characteristic of conversation is to develop the text by 'agreement', and hence the textual strategies employed by the participants are exemplification, (minor) modification, reformulation, and development, of the previous speaker's text. There is the further evidence of support, in the *Hm, a Hm* (lines 11, 18), indicating comprehension, interest, agreement. And while conversations are interactional, there are few or no formal features designed expressly to push the interactional aspect of the occasion. Of course I am not suggesting that the actuality of (all) conversations is agreement; in fact most or many conversations are marked by disagreement, and by absence of support. Conversations, like all texts, are motivated by difference. What I am saying is that in its overt form the genre conversation demands that these characteristics are adhered to. Once they are not, for instance when overt disagreement determines the mode of the interaction, we are dealing with a different genre, perhaps an ARGUMENT or, in more formal cases, a DEBATE. At any rate, it is clear that the forms and functions of the social occasion and the purposes of the participants are what give rise to this particular genre, and those meanings are part of the genre conversation. Competent users of

See Kress (1982) and Halliday in *Spoken and Written Language* (1989).

language are entirely familiar with and very sensitive to the forms and meanings of genre, and it is not uncommon for the question of generic mode to become raised as an issue 'Oh well, I thought we were just having a conversation; if it's an argument you want . . . '.

An interview

	Max	This is for a radio program that I'm doing John ah . . . um . . . Two questions that you can answer briefly the first is what would you say language is, what is language?
	John	What is language?
5	Max	Yeah
	Sid	Communication.
	John	Well it's a it's a it's a different form **yeah** it is communication
	Max	Communication
	John	What do you mean from different people from all over the
10		world?
	Max	Yeah
	John	What would you say language is that? It's just ah haha Jesus Christ that's that's that's something you take for granted I don't know
15	Max	Yeah? What would you say it's made out of?
	John	Noises . . . different noises
	Max	Terrific thanks a lot
	John	I don't know it . . . it . . it's a question . . . it's very hard to . . . what would **you** say language is?
20	Sid	Well it's made out of . . .
	John	What what what is language?
	John	-ation
	Sid	Language is communication between people that . . . but language instigated bullshit that's where it all came from you
25		couldn't talk there wouldn't be so much bullshit around it . . . it's between people of a . . . it's a . . . communication between people
	John	Sounds, Yeah
	Max	That's wonderful thanks a lot
30	John	Ha ha ha
	Sid	That's very interesting

The INTERVIEW is also a genre within speech, and therefore some of the same syntactic/textual forms are present; for instance lines 24–29. Here, in contrast to the conversation, the interactional nature of the occasion is much more foregrounded, and a number of formal features are present to structure that interaction. One is the use of questions of a certain kind by the interviewer, that is questions which have the force of commands *What is language?*, i.e. 'Tell me your view on language'. The interview also uses other forms which have the force of a command, for instance, *Two questions that you can answer briefly* . . . i.e. 'Answer these two questions briefly!' or, in an attempt to close the interview, line 17, *Terrific thanks a lot* and line 29 *That's wonderful thanks a lot*. In an interview, turns are taken at the instigation of the interviewer, who indicates also what the interviewee's turn is to be

22

'about'. Although this particular example is one where the participants know each other reasonably well, and the interviewees were doing the interviewer a favour, in other words, where the interviewer did not have excessive power, nevertheless, by virtue of his role he has a degree of control. That control is somewhat less than in interviews where greater power lies with the interviewer. So for instance, the interviewee feels free to ask 'follow-up' or clarificatory questions—in interviews marked by more power difference that tends to be the case less or not at all. Here the interviewee is prepared to override the interviewer's closing-off signal, and indeed another participant enters in, unbidden. In fact he has 'the last word'. In other words, this interview is constantly teetering on the edge of becoming a conversation. Nevertheless, the formal characteristics of the genre of interview are entirely clear. One crucial one is that the form of the text of the interview is overtly motivated by difference, and is not developed by 'agreement' but by 'direction'. The textual strategies are direction and questioning, on the part of the interviewer, and response, information, and definition, on the part of the interviewee.

As in the case of the conversation, the forms and functions of the social occasion and the purposes of the participants clearly give form and meaning to this genre, and are reflected and encoded in it. It may be important at this stage to pause and note that without the notion of text it would not be possible to differentiate between these two genres; that is, at the level of the clause (or clause-chains and sentences) it is not possible to differentiate. It is when we look at the manner in which clauses are organised in text, via discursive organisation and generic form, that the difference becomes apparent, and it becomes possible to establish their connection with social structures and processes.

Let us now look at one example of a lesson, and see how its generic form compares with those of conversation and interview.

Without the notion of text it would not be possible to differentiate between genres.

A lesson

Lovely things

Teacher: Well we're going to have another look at some of the things we did first um when we first started we found out that we're going to learn our humanities mostly through our senses. How many senses do we have?

5   Child: Five

Teacher: Danny

Child: Five

Teacher: Right we have five. Who's going to tell me what they are yes

Child: Seeing

10 Teacher: Seeing

Child: Smelling

Teacher: Yes

Child: Tasting

Teacher: Yes

15 Child: Hearing

Teacher: Yes

Child: Feeling

23

Teacher: Good boy five senses and we're going to do some work
looking at all of those senses aren't we? We've looked at
20   seeing and now we're looking at hearing. Tell me some of the
lovely things we saw with our sense of sight. Yes. Oh come on
what lovely things can you see yes
Child: Flowers
Teacher: Flowers
25 Child: Birds
Teacher: Right
Child: Paintings
Teacher: Right
Child: Kittens
30 Teacher: Right
Child: Um flowers
Teacher: Oh we've had those. Yes

(G. R. Kress, *Learning to Write*, Routledge and Kegan Paul, London, 1982,
pp.43–4)

Clearly not all LESSONS are alike so that this text is not identical
with all lesson texts; there is variation between teachers, between subject
areas, and variation and change across the years of schooling. Nevertheless I suggest that this text is quite characteristic of generic features
shared by most, perhaps all lessons. Anyone will be able to match their
own experience against my description. This genre has features in
common with conversation and with interview, above all features of
speech, and its interactional nature. It is closer to the genre of interview
than to that of conversation. There is, as in the interview, a great
differential in power, and this is used by the teacher to control and
structure the interaction. Like the interview, this genre is motivated
by difference, a difference of knowledge and power—which here are
entirely interrelated, both dependent on each other. The formal features
which are used to structure the interaction are even more foregrounded
than in the interview : questions and commands are used, as are 'scene
settings' (note the similarity of the opening of the interview and of the
lesson from this point of view: *This is for a radio program that I'm
doing, John* and *Well we're going to have another look at some of the
things . . .*) which serve to focus the (interviewee's and) pupil's attention.

The teacher controls the content in a manner which goes beyond
the interviewer's structuring : the difference lies in their respective
stances towards the information they are seeking. The interviewer is
interested in and usually does not know the information; the teacher
is interested not in the information, which she or he already knows,
but in the pupil's performance/utterance of this information. Unlike
the interviewer, who 'accepts' the information (note the interviewer's
Yeah's and the echoing *Communication*), the teacher 'validates' the
information as well as accepting it. So, line 8: *Right we have five*; line
10: *Seeing*; lines 12, 14, 16: *Yes*; lines 26, 28, 30: *Right*; etc. The
yes's and *right's* also have the further function of 'nominating' the par-
ticipant/respondent, so that the teacher not only controls the content,
and the sequence of interaction, but also controls who is to be a participant. She (in this case) does this by indicating, pointing out a particular student who is to respond. In doing so she also distributes
valuations of knowledge, because when the answer does not correspond

24

to her schema she passes from child to child until she reaches an answer/child which does correspond to her schema. At that point she pauses with some extending remark.

The lesson differs from conversation and interview, perhaps most obviously in the roles which the participants take in the interaction. In a conversation the participants all speak 'on their own behalf' and take turns on their own initiative, without being directed by any one member of the group. That is, the distribution of power in the interaction is such that the genre of conversation does not provide for any one participant to assume a differentiated directing role. In the interview the distribution of power in the interaction is such that the genre provides for strictly differentiated roles. The two—usually—participants may, but don't necessarily, speak on 'their own behalf'. That is, the interviewer may speak on behalf of others, perhaps the audience in a radio or television interview, or of an institution in a job interview. Similarly, the interviewee may speak on someone else's behalf. Turns are taken at the direction of one participant. In interviews with more than two participants, it is usually the role of interviewer which is a multiple one. In a lesson there is power difference between the participants, with the single participant, the teacher, holding greater power over the generally multiple student participants. In addition to the directing function of the interviewer, the teacher 'nominates' which individual is to be the interactant. Consequently, the linguistic forms differ between interview and lesson, generally speaking in these directions:

1 the teacher uses direct commands more frequently (this includes syntactic forms which have assumed, by convention, the force of command, for instance, 'nominations' such as *yes, Danny*);
2 the student's response is more narrowly confined or constructed in and by the teacher's questions;
3 the teacher 'validates' information rather than accepting it—a point where difference of power and of knowledge coincide; interviewers may question further but do not, generally, 'validate' the interviewee's response;
4 the teacher occasionally provides a summary of the information as an end, or a prelude to an episode in the interaction;
5 modalities differ sharply in interviews and in lessons : in interviews power tends to be concealed more than in lessons;
6 while some interviews permit interviewees to ask questions, indeed certain interviews have a formalised section where the interviewee is encouraged to ask questions, the lesson is a genre where one participant cannot ask questions—other than 'confirmatory' questions, *um flowers*, i.e. 'Is "flowers" the correct answer?'.

The general point that emerges here is that an increasing power difference in the social occasion of interaction has specific effects on the nature of the text, which are coded in the respective genres. In a conversation, the genre with least or no power difference, the mechanisms of interaction are formally least foregrounded, and content—the substance of the interaction—is formally most foregrounded. In the lesson, the genre with the most power difference, the mechanism of the interaction is formally more foregrounded and

Increasing power difference in the social occasion of interaction has specific effects on the nature of the text.

25

content is formally least emphasised. That at least is the situation when one looks at the formal features of the genre, and what aspects of the occasion they serve. In the case of the lesson in particular, this results in a paradox; that is, the educational genre *par excellence* turns out not to be about content, but about features directed towards the interaction, towards control and power. The genre which is most distant from educational genres, and which is formally least about power, the conversation, is formally most about content.

The relative 'closedness' or 'openness' of the interaction, itself a feature of power difference, has its correlation in the generic form and in the linguistic features of the resultant text. Here the situation is that the greater the power difference, the more closed the interaction; the less the power difference, the more open the interaction.

To conclude this section I will analyse some examples of another educational genre, the genre of TEXTBOOK. As always, in considering any genre, it is necessary to bear in mind the total interconnectedness of features of the social occasion and features of the genre. The first example that I wish to discuss comes from a history textbook for first year high school students.

Egypt: 9 pyramids

Royal monuments

The pyramids of Egypt are huge funeral monuments built for kings and queens.

The Egyptians believed in life after death for important people. The royal person's body had to be preserved if he was to live happily in the next world. The pyramid would be a safe place for the royal body to lie.

It was believed that the pharaoh was going on a journey in the next world. All the things needed for a journey were piled into the pyramid—transport, food, weapons and treasure.

The pyramid was built to be safe from robbers. Even though every care was taken it seems that every pyramid was broken into and robbed in ancient times.

The pyramid workers

Hundreds of thousands of labourers worked on each pyramid. There are many different views on who these labourers were.

One view is that they worked under the whip. They may have been slaves captured in foreign wars. They may have been Egyptian citizens forced to work by cruel pharaohs.

Another view is that free citizens volunteered their labour. Each year, during the flood, farmers couldn't go near their lands. If they believed that having good crops depended on the well-being of the pharaoh they might have been happy to take part in such an amazing project.

Some of the workers left graffiti on the stones. They worked in gangs and sometimes wrote the name of their gang. Examples found include *the vigorous gang, craftsman crew, the powerful white crown of Khufu* and the *how vigorous is Snofru* gang.

There are other ideas worth thinking about. It is said that such a large number of people could not be forced to work for such a long period.

Another idea is that the labourers began as volunteers. As the project took longer they became tired and then were forced to labour.

Pyramid construction

The ancient Egyptians left no written records which tell about how the pyramids were built. All we can do is look at the pyramids themselves and try to guess how they might have been constructed. There are one or two wall pictures which have helped.

Herodotus talks about machinery used for lifting. There is no other evidence, so scholars don't think it is likely. Most scholars agree that the stones were dragged along with ropes and levered into position. Wooden rollers might have been used in difficult situations. Water may have been used as a lubricant.

Most scholars agree that the stones were pulled up ramps. Some early theories were that one long ramp was used. As the pyramid became taller the ramp became steeper.

Scientists are beginning to reveal the inside structure of the pyramids. There is a central core of rock and rubble. Outside this are buttress walls of carefully cut stone. These walls slope inwards to hold the pyramid together. Some scholars think the pyramids were built a layer at a time.

Kurt Mendelssohn thinks that the wall and core would have gone up first. He says that the builders needed a point in the air. Such as a long pole on top of the centre of the core. If they didn't have this how could they have kept the pyramid to a perfect shape?

(G. Garden, *Life B.C.*, Heinemann Educational Australia, 1980, p. 44)

The larger social context is that of the education system; and within that, the context is that of the structures and interactive processes that constitute the teaching and learning of a particular curriculum area—history—in the early years of high school. A number of features of that situation enter the constitution of this genre: the writer's perception of his task (which is itself a construct of the education system at large), his perception of the discipline and of its constitution, his perception of his audience. Certain features of this genre derive particularly from that latter factor. So for instance the general layout of the text seems designed for an audience which is assumed to have a limited interest in history and a limited ability to concentrate on extended texts, for whom therefore the text needs to be visually (and conceptually) segmented in a certain way. The syntax shows the same effect: generally the writer has aimed to produce sentences with little or no subordination or embedding, that is, he tends to use sentences which have the surface form of single clauses. In other words, the writer has a particular notion of syntactic complexity and of what kinds of complexity an eleven-year-old is capable of mastering. (The fact that in many cases there is 'hidden' complexity, as for instance in the 'reduced' relative-passive clause represented by *captured in foreign wars—They may have been slaves captured in foreign wars*—is not here to the point.) Generally speaking too, the writer tends to use the active rather than the passive voice, and in particular he tends to avoid agentless passives. This may be due to a notion that his audience is one which needs 'liveliness of style', and the assumption that (agentless) passives give the

27

text a more abstract, lifeless feel.

One particular feature is the inclusion of fairly direct instructions/directions in the text. The last paragraph of the section titled 'Pyramid workers' and of the section 'Pyramid construction' each give an example: *There are other ideas worth thinking about*—i.e. 'think of some other ideas', and *If they didn't have this, how could they have kept the pyramid to a perfect shape?*—i.e. 'discuss other means whereby . . .'. This strategy of including direct instructions or questions in the text is quite characteristic of the genre and is a sign of its function, that is, to serve quite explicit didactic purposes.

Despite these features, which are aimed at 'simplification', the text is written within 'scientific discourse', broadly speaking. That discourse has a number of reasonably well understood features. For instance, it tends towards impersonality and the avoidance of any personal constructions. This accords with the broad ideology of science, in which 'objectiveness' and 'factualness' determine that the individual scientist/writer/experimenter is not significant and is merely an (irrelevant) servant of objectively established truth.

Some features of the text mark it as 'scientific'.

Similarly, scientific discourse demands that hypotheses are treated as distinctively different to theories, so that modalities are used to mark that which is portrayed as objectively known (theory) from that which is still the subject of speculation and doubt (as hypothesis). Given that the writer operates with a notion of 'simplification' and yet wishes to remain within the constraints of scientific discourse, he has to adjust the demands of that discourse to the assumed needs of his audience. The writer achieves this by handling impersonality in a manner thought by him appropriate to his readers. Hence there are forms such as *One view is, There are many different views, Another view is, There are other ideas, Another idea is, it seems that, scholars don't think it is likely, Most scholars agree, Scientists are beginning*. There are also some of the agentless passives characteristic of adult genres in this discourse: *It was believed that, Examples found, It is said*. These latter forms, usually predominant in scientific texts, are here far outnumbered by clauses in the active voice.

The modalities signal, as they do in texts written for adult readers, the distance proper to hypothetical statements. In form they again tend to differ from those of adult texts. So certain mental process verbs are used here which would not usually be found in scientific texts written for adults, especially for adult scientists. *It was believed, it seems that, scholars don't think it is likely, some scholars think the, Kurt Mendelssohn thinks that*. This text shares with other scientific texts the use of modal auxiliaries: *They may have been, they might have been happy, such a large number of people could not, All we can do, how they might have been constructed, wooden rollers might have, Water may have been*.

As significant as the use of these modal forms is the use of the so-called present tense to give a contrasting modality, that of certainty, to those parts of the text which are presented as established fact. *The pyramids of Egypt are, There are many different views, Another view is, There are other ideas, It is said, Another idea is, All we can do is look . . . and try, Herodotus talks, Most scholars agree, There is a central core, These walls slope inwards.* This modal form (the so-called present tense) here has two functions: to give the status of 'fact' to the scientific activity going on at the present, and to give the status of 'fact' to certain statements made by scientists working in this area.

A description of the formal features of genre is a description of the total system of all the linguistic features operating in a text. That is, a genre is not characterised by one or two or half a dozen particular linguistic features, but by the totality of the linguistic forms selected in the production of a text. That may seem as though genre cannot be distinguished from text as such, or from the operation of discourses in a text which, in their turn, utilise all the linguistic forms of which the text consists. However, it is clear that linguistic features can serve different functions at one and the same time. Here in this text for instance a form such as *Another view is*, serves the generic function of presenting impersonality in an 'accessible' form; and that form also serves the function of presenting the discursively determined characteristic of 'impersonality'. Discourse determines what is to be said—in this case 'impersonality'; genre determines how it will be said in a contextually determined form. Discourse and genre are discrete factors despite the fact that both are constantly present together in linguistic form. For instance, if the major discourse operating in a text were religious discourse, the generic demands would still produce quite similar effects ; ranging from the layout, to the (assumedly) simplified syntax, to the realisation of discursive demands in a (seemingly) appropriate form for the eleven-year-old reader.

As a contrast and for comparison here is another text from a secondary school textbook. The curriculum area this time is geography.

Regions

The area round a town in which its urban functions exert a strong influence can be described as a *functional region*. In highly urbanised countries this is probably the most useful way of division of large areas into smaller units for study. We need to remember, however, that the boundary of a region can be defined precisely only in terms of one factor, and then only if that factor can be expressed as a quantity. We can talk of part of northern New South Wales as within the region of 50 per cent or more commerical orientation to Brisbane; we can also talk of that part where 50 per cent or more of the people take in Brisbane daily newspapers; the boundaries are different, but they both mean something precise. To speak of the 'Brisbane region' without any indication of the way it is defined is vague indeed. In Chapter 2 the boundary of a population density region was defined from statistics in a precise way.

We have seen too that functional regions overlap and nest one within another. The fringe zones of the four New Zealand towns in Fig. 5.8 would overlap one another if plotted on one map. If the criteria used had been comparison rather than convenience goods, it is probable that all four towns would have come within the functional region of Hamilton, a much larger town. Hamilton, in turn, in other fields could be considered part of the functional region of Auckland, the largest city in New Zealand.

Geographers have at different times thought of regions in different ways. Functional regions round towns as nodes are one kind, applicable in most places, but specially suited to industrial and commercial areas. French geographers early this century considered that a region was a part of the . . .

(D.D. Harris & I.R. Stehbens, *Settlement Patterns and Processes*, Longman Cheshire, Melbourne, 1981, p. 157.)

There are both differences and similarities; and the differences are not random, but are systematically variant versions of the features described above. That is, we are very much within the same broad genre, but specific situational factors have brought about predictable, systematic differences. Layout, for a start, is not organised as in Pyramids, due to a different perception both of the discipline (it is a discipline which is presented as relatively 'harder') and a different perception of the audience, as one who will read a more densely constructed/displayed visual text. This difference carries on, predictably, to the syntax. There is no extensive attempt at 'simplification', and subordination and embedding are common. Passives, including agentless passives, are more frequent here than in the Pyramid text. Active sentences too are frequent. In the Pyramid text active sentences tend to have animate subjects: *labourers worked on each pyramid, free citizens volunteered, the workers left graffiti, Most scholars agree*. In fact that is the rule in the Pyramid text: physical action verbs and mental process verbs take human subject nouns. This is in line with the apparent motive of the writer to write in a 'lively' manner. In the Regions text there is no such rule: *its urban functions exert a strong influence, the boundaries . . . mean something precise, functional regions overlap and nest one within another*.

Like the Pyramid text, Regions contains explicit instructions. These are of two kinds. One, which I will discuss in detail in Chapter 2, instructs the reader to 'be' the scientist: *The area . . . can be described* (described by the reader), *the boundary . . . can be defined, We need to remember* (where the coercively inclusive we instructs the reader to identify with the text), and so on. The insistent use of the *we* is a generic feature which signals a different relation to the audience; that audience is here regarded as ready, suited to, and able to be identified with geographers, that is, the audience is seen as far enough along the path towards induction into the discipline to be included in the text, or to consider itself in that light.

Again, the Regions text is written within scientific discourse. Impersonality and objectivity are signalled in broadly similar ways to the Pyramid text, though appropriately adapted to this differing discipline and audience. Agentless passives are a prominent form, as are nominals of the kind of which *division* (*the most useful way of division*) is an example. Similarly with a form such as *To speak of the 'Brisbane region'* where the subject of the verb *to speak* is left implicit, so that no personal noun need appear. The use of the we may seem to be an exception, though it seems in fact to signal 'the community of scientific geographers' and hence remains an impersonal form. Modalities have the same function here as in the Pyramid text, though with predictable variations from the Pyramid text. So for instance, forms such as *One view is, scholars don't think it is likely* do not occur here. The modal auxiliary *can* is most frequent, *could* occurring only once. These are complemented by the modal adverbs and adjectives *probably, probable*. But above all, the form which distinguishes Regions from Pyramids in modality is the hypothetical/logical modality *if . . . then*, and *. . . then only if . . . .* As in Pyramids these modalities of probability are set against the modality of certainty of the so-called present tense form which is more prominent here than in the Pyramids text, particularly in conjunction with the verb *to be*: *this is probably, can be defined . . . only, is vague indeed, it is probable, Functional regions . . . are one kind.* Unlike Pyramids, the Regions text is characterised by a further generic feature, the use of specialist technical/scientific terms: *urban functions, functional region, highly urbanised countries, factor, the region of 50 per cent . . . commercial orientation to Brisbane, the 'Brisbane region', nest.* In some cases the writers have marked this shift into specialist vocabulary by italicising certain forms.

The sources of texts

Here I wish to sum up briefly the elements of the discussion in this chapter. I said that texts are the relevant units of language, if our interest in language goes beyond the merely formalistic to any of the concerns of social, cultural, educational questions. The forms and meanings of texts are determined by discourses—systems of meanings arising out of the organisation of social institutions—and by genres—formal conventional categories whose meanings and forms arise out of the meanings, forms and functions of the conventionalised occasions of social interactions. Clearly, both of these sources of the forms and meanings of texts are entirely social and cultural. Nor are discourses and genres unrelated—social institutions tend to have their own particular occasions of interaction, and so it seems at times that when we are talking about genre we are talking about discourse, and talking about characteristics of discourse when we are discussing genre. Clearly too, certain discourses tend to have preferred relations with certain genres, and some genres are incompatible with certain discourses.

Texts are given form and meaning by discourse and genre. Nevertheless texts are the product of individual speakers who, as social agents, are themselves formed in discourses through texts, attempting to make sense of the competing, contradictory demands and claims of differing discourses. The history of each individual traces her or his passage through, and experience of, a variety of discourses, not haphazardly encountered, but experienced in the contexts of specific social structures and processes. For each individual therefore her or his discursive history is itself a history of contradiction, tension, mismatching incompatibilities. Each individual exists in a particular **set** of discursive forms deriving from the social institutions in which she or he finds herself or himself. The resolution of these tensions, contradictions, and incompatibilities, provides a constant source of dialogue, and hence of text—whether silently spoken or spoken aloud to oneself, or carried out in dialogue with another.

31

No one individual's discursive history can be exactly that of another, no matter how similar their personal and social histories. Add to this the differential social placing of any one as a social being, and it is clear that while social beings share much, they also are, in any one particular instance, on any one given occasion divided by differences, of whatever kind. This difference always has linguistic form, and leads to dialogue, and hence to text. Texts are constructed in and by this difference. Where there is no difference there is silence. In texts the discursive differences are negotiated, governed by differences in power, which are themselves in part encoded in and determined by discourse and by genre. No text is ever the text of a single speaker or writer. All texts show the traces of differing discourses, contending and struggling for dominance. Texts are therefore the sites of struggle, always, and in being the sites of struggle, texts are the sites of linguistic and cultural change. Individuals, as social agents and constructed in discourse, are the bearers and the agents of that struggle.

No text is ever the work of any one person.

Individuals as social agents are the bearers and agents of struggle and of change.

32

Chapter 2

Speech and speakers: the formation of individuals in discourse and genre

Our experience of language is the experience of texts. In texts the resources of language are always organised in systematic ways deriving from the structures and processes of the social occasions in which the text originated. Consequently, our knowledge of language is the knowledge of all the texts that we have experienced and the social settings in which we experienced them as a participant, whether as reader or hearer, or as speaker or writer, in specific roles assigned to us in those texts.

The knowledge that any one individual has of language is therefore always a partial knowledge, it is knowledge organised in a particular way. And it is, as I tried to show, a knowledge which is likely to differ from individual to individual not on the basis of individualistic characteristics, but on the basis of social factors. In this chapter I wish to explore how the relation of language users to their language is constructed; what the nature of that relation is; how it facilitates and how it constrains linguistic and social behaviour; how it permits or impedes access to social and cultural knowledge and values; and how that relation enables or stifles social effectiveness, and distributes power.

Discourse and readers

Discourses present modes of talking about the world from the point of view of a social institution. One of the most thoroughly studied discourses is that of sexism. Sexist discourse is about the socialisation of the natural category of sex as gender. That socialisation has massively far-reaching effects on all of social life; on families and family structures; on work and lack of work; on leisure; on how men and women are to see themselves and their possibilities of action; on larger scale political structures. In short, there are few areas of social and cultural life which are not affected by the prescriptions of sexist discourse. To give some concreteness to this discussion, here are two further extracts from the article which I have already discussed briefly in Chapter 1, in *Cleo*, June 1984. The article describes different types of women, in the office, and instructs each type how to modify their behaviour in order to improve their situation at work. A number of 'types' are addressed, 'Miss Mouse', 'Miss Seductress', 'Ms Winner', 'Miss Nonchalant', 'Miss Power Broker'. Here are the descriptions of two, 'Miss Seductress' and 'Ms Winner'.

Miss Seductress

There's always one of this type in every gathering: at parties she laughs alluringly and touches everyone (even your man); when meeting men she pouts, flutters eyelashes and makes her body do the talking. Even in the supermarket she totters in high sling backs and wears clingy angora. Yes, she's the one who always believes that everything will come to her as long as she looks gorgeous. She attracts men like bees to the honey pot and keeps their attention by direct eye contact while always flashing a dazzling smile. She's all teeth, luscious lips, glossy hair, painted fingernails and seductive curves. Men love her, even if women don't, and that's just the way she likes it. She's managed to get good jobs in the past (always male bosses) and never has to 'go dutch' on dinner dates. The trouble with Miss Seductress is that half the world is made up of women, and the men who enjoy her type go down on record as having short attention spans. Which leaves her high and dry much of the time.

You, Miss Seductress, need a lot of help. Turn down the sirens for a start—you won't miss out on the men. You may miss out on the bounders, but you could score with Mr. Nice-Guy, the one who's likely to stay for more than the first act. Office harmony hasn't been your strong point because you alienate your female co-workers. Rising in the hierarchy takes enthusiasm and ability, not low cut dresses and knowing looks. Restraint is the key word, in all aspects of your life.

Ms Winner

Ms Winner isn't always easy to categorise at once, because her self-confidence is so unassuming. She's the type who doesn't need to impress others with her abilities—she knows they will shine through anyway. Her self-assurance comes through in every mannerism, every item of clothing, her relaxed posture, her confident speech. She dresses with flair, knowing how to combine basically conservative clothes with innovative extras to form a completely co-ordinated outfit which exudes her personal style. Basically, Ms Winner has panache. She dresses well for the occasion whether it's a job interview or dinner party. Her hair is cut in modern, but not outrageous, style, her makeup is subtle. But Ms Winner's strongest point is her well-modulated conversation which is always lively and intelligent. She has many friends of both sexes who never feel threatened by her. She doesn't talk behind people's backs, but is no sycophant either. She has a mind of her own, but doesn't impose it on others. Ms Winner, you're on the right track, so don't change a thing.

(*Cleo*, June 1984)

'Miss Seductress' is obviously constructed as one kind of stereotype; while it is a half attempted caricature it is also not all that far from the construction of women in sexist discourse in advertisements, short stories, popular novels, and so on. Characteristic descriptions abound: *laughs alluringly, pouts, flutters eye-lashes, clingy angora, gorgeous, luscious lips, glossy hair*, etc. Her mode of behaviour is stereotypical:

34

the female who constructs herself, and the males whom she 'allures', as sex objects. The relationship between genders is constructed as an objectifying, possessive, economic/materialist one, where sex is a commodity like other commodities in a market of human beings. The liberated readers of Cleo are meant to recognise the type and to identify with the disapproving caricature. In other words, the ideal reader is one who is aware of the analyses of sexist discourse provided by feminist critiques (and feminist discourse), and one who identifies with that critique. At least that is the kind of reader constructed by the text in one part. But the text also demands a reader who is worried by men with *short attention spans* and by being left *high and dry much of the time*, who prefers not to *miss out on the men*. The text clearly disapproves of *bounders* and approves of *Mr. Nice-Guy*. In other words in the same text, in the construction of the relationships between men and women, and of a set of values held by the text's ideal reader, we do have sexist discourse—where a woman's role and place is defined by reference to men both as sex objects and desirable material commodities. The reader constructed here is a complex one, one who has to be able to negotiate the contradictions and tensions between a traditional sexist discourse and its values, and a feminist discourse which is present in the text and acts in a mildly subversive fashion.

To expand slightly on this point : the difference which motivates this text is that between the feminist discourse which is the source of the disapproval of aspects of 'Miss Seductress', and the underlying sexist discourse which demands that women should know their place.

The clash of discourses exemplified here is the condition of all texts, given that texts are constituted by and in difference. Generally speaking, the writers/producers of texts attempt to resolve the contradiction. Indeed it is a demand made by most genres that discursive difference should be resolved; texts in which it is not are seen as 'confused', 'inconclusive', 'unsatisfactory'. The task of the writer is therefore that of producing a plausible, coherent reading position, one which seems to transcend the contradictions by a number of strategies—elimination of one discourse, dominance of one over another, or attempts at accommodation. In this example the writer's solution is to appeal to the demands and (potential) rewards of work: the aim of the ideal reader is 'rising in the hierarchy'. The demands of the world of work override the demands of sexual desire, which have to be subordinated to it. That is, a third discourse is introduced in order to dismiss the claims of the absent feminist discourse, and to permit those of sexist discourse to reassert itself. The aims of the discourse of work are themselves constructed in sexist discourse, in the prescriptions of how **men** are to see themselves if they are to be judged as successful. But while for a successful male energy, competitiveness, aggression are perfectly acceptable and even necessary attributes, that is not so for this woman reader. She must not *alienate [her] female co-workers*, and the key word for her is *restraint* not aggression or assertiveness, let alone the competitive killer instinct.

The achievement of this text is to acknowledge the challenge of feminist critique by bringing its statements into the text, and there repositioning that discourse and the reader within traditional sexist discourse.

Successful texts resolve discursive differences.

What are the reader's options? Clearly, she is 'positioned' in a specific way in the text, (though there is a 'he' reader too, who reads the text as a description of what he can expect that women should be). The text constructs its ideal reader by providing a certain 'reading position' from where the text seems unproblematic and 'natural'. The reader may already be that ideal reader. That is, by buying a certain journal, the reader has already positioned herself in a whole system of texts, of genres, of discourses, that is, in a 'reading formation'. The sets of texts which constitute each issue of the magazine (and a series of issues—though here historical changes have to be addressed carefully) both select a certain category of reader and (re-)construct that reader in the process of reading. So the reading subject may already be formed in certain ways and be part of a group defined by their common readership of a set of texts. That is, the reading subject may belong to a reading formation (to quote Bennett once more) 'that set of discursive and intertextual determinations which organise and animate the practice of reading, connecting texts and readers in specific relations to one another in constituting readers as reading subjects of particular types and texts as objects-to-read in particular ways'.

> The reader is 'con-
> structed' in the text.

The reader may not already be the text's ideal reader. One function of texts of this kind is to recruit new readers to a 'reading position'; perhaps a young woman who is becoming a reader of the magazine, or is beginning work. The text attempts to coerce the reader, by its 'obviousness' and 'naturalness', to become its ideal reader, to step into the reading position constructed for the reader in the text. Such coercion may work in the short or in the long term. This is where the insistently repetitive nature of such texts is crucial. It is in constant (re)reading of texts in this or other genres, or texts constructed at the place of work as 'chat', or 'interview', or 'job description', that the assimilating tendency of discourses works, via the reader's activity in reading texts. Of course it seems that anyone may refuse to be an ideal or appropriate reader, or to be a reader at all. However, in my discussion of the reading of textbooks I point out the pressures which are exerted on readers to be ideal readers: in school this happens through the pressures of assessment; at work it happens in pressures towards conformity.

The second section of the extract, 'Ms Winner', announces in its title that we are dealing here with the 'new' woman, someone firmly within a feminist discourse. However it is not hard to see (and now entirely predictable) that 'Ms Winner' is constructed in sexist discourse. A series of negatives (overt and covert) gives the definition of her position and defines—by negation—the position which is being challenged : she is self-confident but she is unassuming; she doesn't need to impress; her qualities will shine through anyway (despite the unassuming manner); she dresses with flair but basically conservatively; she dresses innovatively but in a completely co-ordinated style; she has her hair cut in a modern but not outrageous style; her conversation is well-modulated (not strident, shrill, loud), etc. In other words, Ms Winner has already taken the keyword restraint thoroughly to heart, in all aspects of [her] life. This section of the text therefore confirms the reading position constructed in the 'Miss Seductress' segment.

Both segments have the function of confirming sexist discourse. The 'Miss Seductress' segment uses feminist discourse to check one undesirable aspect of sexist discourse, namely that women, in constructing themselves as sex objects may come to be sexually overly active and aggressive. The 'Ms Winner' segment attempts to check another undesirable possibility of sexist discourse, namely that women may tackle men on the ground constructed and defined for **them** in sexist discourse, of being aggressive, competitive, flamboyant, ruthless—'excessive'. The constantly insistent demands of a discourse, as here for instance the demands of sexist discourse for women to 'be' certain kinds of things, to act in certain ways, have short-term and long-term effects. In the short term a reading position is constructed by a discourse, which provides instructions about how to read a text or a set of texts. That instruction is always also an instruction to act in certain ways, to take stances, to conform or adapt. In the longer term these constantly reiterated demands construct certain 'subject positions', that is, sets of statements which describe and prescribe a range of actions, modes of thinking and being, for an individual, compatible with the demands of a discourse. In that way we learn how to be men or women, husbands or wives, sons or daughters, mothers or fathers, secretaries or bosses, teachers or policemen, lovers, or casual friends.

'Subject positions' are sets of statements which describe and prescribe a range of options one may take up.

Subject positions and reading positions are therefore closely interrelated. Both are established through the operation of discourses in texts.

Genre and reading position

Discourses construct reading positions and subject positions for the readers of texts. Genres similarly construct reading positions. As I pointed out in my discussion of the genres of conversation and of interview in the last chapter, each genre constructs positions or roles which the participants in the genres occupy. I would like to develop further this point of the linguistic construction and positioning of the reader by a more detailed analysis of the textbook example *Regions*.

Regions
The area round a town in which its urban functions exert a strong influence can be described as a *functional region*. In highly urbanised countries this is probably the most useful way of division of large areas into smaller units for study. We need to remember, however, that the boundary of a region can be defined precisely only in terms of one factor, and then only if that factor can be expressed as a quantity. We can talk of part of northern New South Wales as within the region of 50 per cent or more commercial orientation to Brisbane: we can also talk of that part where 50 per cent or more of the people take in Brisbane daily newspapers; the boundaries are different, but they both mean something precise. To speak of the 'Brisbane region' without any indication of the way it is defined is vague indeed. In Chapter 2 the boundary of a population density region was defined from statistics in a precise way.

We have seen too that functional regions overlap and nest one within another. The fringe zones of the four New Zealand towns in Fig. 5.8 would overlap one another if plotted on one map. If the criteria used had been comparison rather than convenience goods, it is probable that all four towns would have come within the functional region of Hamilton, a much larger town. Hamilton, in turn, in other fields could be considered part of the functional region of Auckland, the largest city in New Zealand.

Geographers have at different times thought of regions in different ways. Functional regions round towns as nodes are one kind, applicable in most places, but specifically suited to industrial and commercial areas. French geographers early this century considered that a region was a part of the
. . .

(D.D. Harris & I.R. Stehbens, Settlement Patterns and Processes,
Longman Cheshire, Melbourne, 1981, p. 157)

The social context is that of the education system, of secondary schooling, of the curriculum area of geography and the use of text-books in that. The participants, from the student's point of view, are herself or himself, and a 'them' which at times has the human face of the teacher, and at other times is quite invisible, institutional. The student reader/learner is positioned in the text by a number of linguistic devices, all generally tending in the direction of providing a space which the student/reader is coerced to occupy.

A number of forms have an 'empty' syntactic subject position. Most frequently here it is the agentless passive, that is, a passive form without its agent noun : *can be described, can be defined, can be expressed, it is defined, the criteria used, if plotted.* The empty agent position invites the reader to assume that place, in at least two ways : as the individual child reader, and as a (proleptically constructed) 'budding scientific geographer'. Other subjectless forms are the non-finite *to speak* of the *'Brisbane region'* (where the reader is asked in a similar way to become the speaker/subject); nominal forms such as *most useful way of division*, *units for study* in which the nominal form stands in a clear syntactic relation to a full clause such as 'we can divide this most usefully . . .', '. . . we can study these . . .'.

The insistent use of the pronoun *we* has a similar tendency. It asks the child to identify with and to be one of the group who speak in this way. The use of the modal auxiliary *can* is in this context ambiguously about permission or ability. The permission-reading constructs and positions the child reader in the relatively less powerful role of student who 'is permitted to do . . .'. The ability-reading constructs and positions the child reader in the role of fellow investigator. The verb *need* as in *We need to remember* has a similar function, indicating either compulsion/obligation (we have to . . .), or a shared 'need'.

There are other modality forms which reinforce the second kind of reading. So for instance the emphatic *indeed* in *To speak of the 'Brisbane region' . . . is vague indeed*, where the emphasiser signals disapproval by a covert negation/prohibition of this procedure. The child reader is invited to identify with the disapproval which again positions her or him as carefully meticulous scientist. *Probably* gives a similar invitation : rather than stating a fact and informing the reader, *probably* invites participation by the reader in an act of evaluating a hypothesis.

Cohesive links to previously established and therefore shared knowledge place the reader in a position of identification with the writer. There are several instances : *In Chapter 2 the boundary* where *In Chapter 2* refers to the previously shared activity of reading, and the consequently common knowledge; *We have seen too* where the verb of perception *seen* and the emphasiser *too* both refer to past shared activity and established knowledge. Other verbs, such as *remember* in *We need to remember* have a cohesive, identifying function. Here it is not at all clear that the reference is to an actual shared memory, rather it is a case where the writer imposes the presupposition of shared and common knowledge on the reader.

These lexical and syntactic features position the child as a reader and at the same time construct her or him as a certain kind of reader; in this case a 'fellow scientific geographer'. Other textual/rhetorical devices have largely similar effects. So for instance the use of careful, detailed explanations; the weighing of probabilities; the finely nuanced definitions . . . *only* . . . *and only if* . . ., all these construct the reader in certain ways. The italicised *functional region* (in other texts handled by scare-quotes) signals to the reader that this is a technical term, which has to be attended to, absorbed, remembered.

The construction of a reading position has at least two effects. On the one hand, it positions readers precisely in a text, instructing them what role to assume in reading, what stance to take. On the other hand, it constructs readers as certain kinds of linguistic and social beings. In this latter effect it is quite like the discursive construction of the reader. The construction of the reader in genre is an instruction about who, what, and how to be in a given social situation, occasion, interaction; the construction of the reader in discourse is an instruction to the reader about who, what and how to be in the larger social institutions (rather than on specific occasions **within** those institutions) in which she or he is placed. As an example, the larger social institution may be that of a profession, say medicine, law, or education. That institution has certain characteristic discourses associated with it, which arise out of, give expression to and encode the values, meanings, and practices of that institution. Within that institution there are many differing kinds of conventionalised social occasions : interviews, briefings, reports, lectures, assessments, discussions, etc. These each have their own forms, meanings and purposes. Texts are constructed in and by both discourse and genres; and so are readers. In the text the two intermesh, often inextricably. In a medical interview it seems as though medical discourse and (medical) genre are one, inseparably. However, when we look at interviews outside of the area of medicine, we discover that interviews have significantly similar features, which are due not to discourse but to genre. Similarly when we look at discourse across a range of different texts we find that medical discourse has significantly similar features across a range of genres; these are due therefore not to genre but to discourse.

What is the effect of this process for the reader? What social, cultural, linguistic values and meanings does the student reader learn in this text? He or she learns about the value system, system of norms and modes of behaviour which characterise being 'a geographer', or 'a scientist' more generally. In this the child learns also what kind of social being he or she would need to be in order to be a member of this community. Specifically she or he would learn about being a member of a community which insists on a denial of the significance of the individual member—the impersonality, objectivity of science—the process of theory—construction, setting off the hypothetical from the theoretically established, the need for meticulously careful modes of working. Other forms tend towards confirming the child reader as a subordinate, less powerful participant, as the student who is to be instructed. In other words, the genre encodes and presents a set of possibilities for the reader; possibilities of being a certain kind of social agent with all that entails. The text presents, simultaneously, the resources of language which are necessary in order to be that social agent, organised in a systematic way appropriate to a competent performance of the social linguistic role coded in the genre; and it presents the sets of values, indication of modes of actions and behaviour appropriate to being a competent social agent on a given social occasion.

The politics of reading in schools

Readers need not comply with the demands of a reading position constructed for them. The options range from not being the reader at all, to a distanced, critical reading, where the reader refuses to enter the reading position constructed in the text, and thereby reconstructs the text in a significantly different form in reading it. The task of the writer is to construct a text which will most effectively coerce the reader into accepting the constructed text. To do this, the text should seem natural and plausible, uncontentious—from the reader's point of view—and obvious. Clearly the best reader will be a critical, a resistant reader, one who both sees the constructedness of the text and of the reading position and who can at the same time reconstruct the text in a manner useful to herself or himself. Hence the aim of the teaching of reading in school should be just that : to train effective readers, readers who are active in relation to the text, able to construct the text to their benefit.

Paradoxically, reading in school positively counteracts the engendering of such modes of reading. The extract that I have discussed shows sufficient evidence of coercion into the reading position constructed in the text. The whole weight of the institution tends in that direction. Just as in the lesson the children respond not in order to inform the teacher but in order to demonstrate certain kinds of knowledge, just so in reading children are asked to read not, primarily, in order to learn, but primarily in order to 'comprehend'. To establish my point clearly here is another extract from the same text as the *Regions* extract.

The influence of Brisbane in northern New South Wales
There was at one time a strong agitation in the northern part of New South

Wales to form a new state to be called New England. At the time when Queensland was separated from New South Wales, the boundary originally suggested was latitude 30°S.

Find this line on a map. What towns now in New South Wales would have become part of Queensland? What is the present border (a) in the west, (b) in the east? Why is the eastern part of the present boundary more satisfactory than latitude 30°S, with the possible exception of the coastal strip?

The settlers in New England objected to the 30°S proposal, and the present boundary was chosen. However, the trading influence of Brisbane is strong in northern New South Wales. To find out how strong it was I.R.M. McPhail and E.R. Woolmington did some research, in an area north from Armidale and east from Moree.

Reilly's Law of retail gravitation, from which the breaking point formula was derived, was for the influence of cities A and B on an intervening place C as follows:

$$\frac{\text{Influence of A}}{\text{Influence of B}} = \frac{\text{Population of A}}{\text{Population of B}} \left(\frac{\text{Distance B to C}}{\text{Distance A to C}}\right)^2$$

If we use Grafton as an example, and use 1976 populations and distances in kilometres by road, this becomes

$$\frac{\text{Influence of Sydney at Grafton}}{\text{Influence of Brisbane at Grafton}} = \frac{2765040}{892907} \times \left(\frac{357}{674}\right)^2 = 0.869$$

which in words says that Sydney can expect 46.5 per cent of the trade and Brisbane 53.5 per cent (ratio of 0.869 to 1).

McPhail and Woolmington did this kind of calculation for a number of towns based on 1961 populations. At that time the Brisbane share of Grafton trade was theoretically 51 per cent, suggesting that Brisbane's influence has been increasing. With enough percentages for different towns it was possible to draw a map with isopleths joining places with an equal percentage of expected Brisbane influence. The result is shown in Fig. 5.11.

The researchers next undertook extensive investigation of actual trade by distributing a questionnaire in the main towns of the region. They received the remarkably good result of a 90 per cent return, and so were able to estimate totals of wholesale purchases from Sydney and Brisbane for each town. These results were recorded as in Fig. 5.12 and then mapped in Fig. 5.13.

Name two towns where the actual trade influence of Brisbane was greater, and two where it was smaller, than the theoretical model indicated.

Other tests of Brisbane's influence were also made in the study; for example, passenger flows towards Brisbane (Fig. 5.14), the circulation of Brisbane daily newspapers (Fig. 5.15) and television penetration.

(D.D. Harris & I.R. Stehbens, *Settlement Patterns and Processes*, Longman
Cheshire, Melbourne, 1981, p.154.)

The text contains direct instructions to the child reader : *Find this line on a map, What towns now in New South Wales, What is the present border.* Or later : *Name two towns*, or in parts not reproduced here : *Draw a sketch map, Can you suggest a reason.* What is remarkable about this is that direct command, and information, are presented in the same text without any transition, as though they were qualitatively the same. The point of course is that they are. The text is about 'instruction', both in the sense of 'commanding to do' and in the sense of 'informing about', and the two are here (presented as) identical. All parts of the text instruct in this ambiguous sense (or rather, in this sense which is ambiguous for the distanced and resistant reader, but which is not ambiguous for the coerced reader, for the schoolchild reader for instance). It is a neat example of the identity of knowledge and power in the education system. The significance is that the student reader is not permitted to be a critical, a resistant reader.

Education should produce critical, resistant readers.

If my aim of educating resistant readers is accepted as being an appropriate and necessary one—and I believe that most educators do have that as their aim—then strategies need to be thought about which will enable children to learn as critical readers. A first step would seem to be to tackle the ambiguity of 'instruction', and to dissolve it into its components of 'informing' and 'commanding'. In other words, my own goals are not about the abolition of structure, of hierarchy, or of power, but rather about the demystification which would make clear when either of the two modes were being used.

The reader's construction of meaning

To what extent is my analysis about the kind of reader which the geography text constructs, part of the meaning of that text? Given that the author/writer of that text presumably did not consciously express that meaning in the text, there are two answers. Both are implicit in what I have been saying so far. On the one hand, discourses and genres exercise their influence on the writer, so that no writer writes (or speaker speaks) outside the forms and meanings of discourse and of genre. To some, in fact a significant, extent therefore the genre and the discourses construct the meaning of a text, irrespective of the writer. The author/writer is to that extent a scribe obeying the demands of discourse and of genre. Readers are not passive on the other hand and contribute in various ways to the meaning of a text, in the act of reconstruction of the text, which is what reading is.

Readers who adopt the reading position coded in the text by discourse and genre perform an act of reconstruction which is least subversive of the text. Nevertheless even such readers will differ in important respects, have different discursive histories, different present social positions to those of the writer, and to the writer's coded reading position. Furthermore, each reader reads a text in a specific context which structures the reading to some extent. All of that is obvious, and important. What it means is that no text is ever merely absorbed, passively, by some inactive, inert reader. And consequently every reading involves some reconstitution of the text.

Resistant readers clearly reconstruct texts in more far-reaching ways. Such readings are made possible by distance of some kind. It might be the distance provided by a different discourse, or by the fact that the reader is not positioned by the genre. The textbook extract may serve as an example : any reader who is not part of the social occasion of which this text is a part and a result, and of which this genre is an encoding, will not find himself positioned as a reader. In other words, given that texts occur on specific social occasions which provide identified places for the participants, then a text read outside of that occasion is read with that distance. A reader who 'occupies' a discourse which contrasts with or contradicts the discourses appearing in a given text clearly will resist the reading position provided by the text, and consequently reconstruct the text from the point of the contrasting discourse. A feminist reader is likely to reconstruct the 'Miss Seductress' and 'Ms Winner' texts in the way that I have done here. Whereas for the ideal reader the meaning of that text might be about 'advice for getting on better at work', for the resistant reader the meaning of the text might be about 'confirming women in their subordinate place in a male-dominated world'.

Those are very different readings, and lead to very different actions. What I would like to explore here is the question of the limits of the reconstruction, and 'rereading of texts'. Beyond that I wish to address a common response to this kind of analysis, which is along the lines that a text can mean anything, 'it just depends on your personal opinion'. My answers to both points are largely similar. If the meaning of texts is constructed in genre and in discourse, then the reconstruction of the text equally takes place in genre and in discourse. One limiting factor to a rereading is therefore the set of genres and discourses available to a reader, within which a text can be reread. There is at any one time a finite set of genres and discourses within a given social group, only some of which may be available to a reader. These provide one set of limits within which reading can take place.

But beyond this, the text itself imposes limitations on its reading, on its reconstruction. For instance, the interview which I discussed above could, without too much difficulty be reread as a conversation; to a reader who brings certain discourses of authority to the reading of this text the relative absence of power difference could be read as a sign of the genre of conversation. And perhaps the lesson could be reread as a peculiar kind of interview. The interview can also be seen to have some features of a lesson, and could be read in that way. But it would, I suggest, be impossible for readers in our society to read the conversation as a lesson, or vice versa. In other words, there are formal features in a genre which resist being reconstructed beyond a certain point, and thereby impose specific limits on possibilities of reading and reconstruction of the text. Similarly, there are features of the discourses operating in a text which set limits to reading and reconstruction. I have discussed this in relation to the *Cleo* text; it, for instance, could not be read as a text constructed within religious discourse, without doing massive violence to the text; such a reading would lack plausibility.

Reading as reconstruction of the text is an ideological activity, an attempt to reconstruct a text emanating from one ideological position as a different text, which may be seen as subversive of its former function (e.g. my readings of the *Cleo* extracts and the textbook example), or which may be used to support a new or differing ideological position. Much of literary criticism is a reading of that kind, reconstructing focal texts in order to dislodge them from one ideological position, to subvert that position, and to use the texts to construct a new or buttress an existing tradition. It is this ideological work which drives the practice of literary criticism, and gives such significance to that institution. A quite similar process is at work in the discipline of history, and in the writing of history. It too is essentially a rereading of sets of texts in the service of some ideological motive. Translations, transcriptions, summaries, synopses, 'stylistic alterations' are all rereadings and reconstructions whose ideological force is not that difficult to analyse and describe.

See Fowler, Hodge, Kress & Trew (1979).

Readings are not motivated by 'just personal opinion', though to the individual reader that is certainly how it appears. He or she has a certain discursive history, and knowledge of genres, and is located within a set of discourses—related to factors such as class, race, gender, age. It is the particular combination of these factors in **interaction with** the text which leads to any given reading. So although from the individual's point of view her or his reading is 'just my personal opinion' that personal opinion is socially constructed. While there are therefore a very large number of readings, perhaps an infinite number, the kinds of readings are not at all random, anarchic, unprincipled or merely individualistic. For me, this is an important point to insist on; and the contrast of a potentially infinite number of readings and the social (discursive and generic) determination of readings turns out to be entirely explicable and inevitable; and not at all paradoxical.

Speech and writing: the spheres of the private and the public

Differences between spoken and written language are discussed at length by M.A.K. Halliday in *Spoken and Written Language* (1989).

The two modes in which language occurs, speech and writing, make fundamentally different uses of the resources of the linguistic system. Certain of these differences are obvious: writing cannot rely on those features which depend on sound—such as stress, rhythm, and above all, intonation. Nor can writing draw on those extra-verbal signals which are so integral to and integrated with spoken interactions. The meanings carried in speech by intonation have to be translated into the sequential, syntactic possibilities of written language. As in any translation, many such meanings are dependent on the resources of one mode (or language) and cannot be translated into another mode (or language). Novelists attempt to capture the qualities of speech in the transliterated/translated forms of writing. Here are a few examples from Joseph Conrad's *Typhoon*:

'Got to pick up the dollars'. He appealed to Mr. Rout, smiling pitifully at random. 'What's that?' asked Mr. Rout, wildly. 'Pick up . . .? I don't care . . .'. Then quivering in every muscle, but with an exaggeration of paternal tone, 'Go away now, for God's sake'. . . . The boatswain yelled excitedly : 'Come along. Get the mate out. He'll be trampled to death. Come on'. . . . 'Leave me alone—damn you. I am all right', screeched Jukes.

(J. Conrad, *Typhoon*, Heinemann, London, 1903, pp. 78, 80, 81)
[emphasis added]

44

Beyond the difference of resources are others, deriving from the social situations in which speech and writing occur, and which have themselves settled into conventional form. Above all, it is the differential use of the clause as the basic textual unit which marks speech off from writing. Broadly speaking, the organisation of clauses in casual, informal speech is a linear, sequential one, one of clause-chains, tending towards co-ordination, either by conjunctions such as *and*, *or*, *but*, *then*, *when*, *that* (with and generally speaking being the most frequent) or by intonational means. In writing the organisation of clauses is hierarchical, within sentences, where clauses are subordinated, embedded, nominalised. As a fairly characteristic example of speech here is part of a taped and transcribed interview:

See Kress (1982) and Halliday (1989).

Interview

See we went through this in '81 and I was one of the officials that were involved . . . er once we'd worked out the severance side of things we were gonna have to deal with the people who wanted to relocate and . . . they said to management we had hardship . . . management rejected it . . . then we had to go through a series of interviews with people at the plant level . . . to er so they could tell us what their hardship was and I found that was er pretty abhorrent to me because er you were dealing with some very personal problems er . . . that people and I didn't want to know it as a trade union official and I don't think they wanted to tell me . . . er they were certainly more prepared to tell me as a union official than they were management people . . . but that's what busted down er and we told management we're not going to set ourselves up as God . . . and er no one should . . . and er that's how we came about in er 1981 to have this hardship unqualified . . . interesting thing is that management's now . . . in 1984 at arbitration proceedings the other week . . . er come up with the term er elected self redundancy what a shocking sort of termination term that is eh?

This kind of clausal structure is characteristic of casual informal speech. The significance of this structuring from the point of view of my argument here lies in the kinds of possibilities that it offers in a number of connected areas, particularly in cognitive, conceptual, social and political terms. The point I wish to make essentially concerns the close interconnection of modes of thinking with the structures of public, social and political life. A comparison of speech structures with writing structures may help to make this clearer. Take a section from this extract (1) *we were gonna have to deal with the people* (2) *who wanted* (3) *to relocate and . . .* (4) *they said to management* (5) *we had hardship* . . . (6) *management rejected it . . .* (7) *then we had to go through a series of interviews with people at the plant level . . .* (where . . . indicates pause/hesitation). The sequential, one-at-a-time clause structure mirrors a conceptual structure whose logic is that of sequenced, additive development. For instance the sequence from clause 4 to clause 7 is entirely that of temporal succession. The complexity of the argument—it is a complex argument—has to be developed by successive addition. A written form of this argument would be constructed entirely differently. For a start the basic unit would be a (multi-clausal) sentence,

45

in which the ordering of the clauses would be determined by and would reflect a conceptual structure whose logic would be that of a hierarchy reflecting conceptual (and, beyond that rhetorical, social and political) priorities. A typical translation into writing might be something like 'Management rejected an approach by a group of employees who had requested relocation on the grounds of hardship'. In this hypothetical version two things have happened: several clauses have been transformed into nominal (noun-like) forms, e.g. *approach, relocation*; other clauses have been integrated into the single hierarchical sentence structure, in a structure of main and subordinate, embedding and embedded clauses.

Writing has a structuring logic which differs fundamentally from that of speech. It is a logic of the nominal rather than of the verbal; of objects rather than processes; of abstraction rather than specificness/concreteness; a logic of hierarchy and of integration rather than a logic of sequence and addition. Western technological societies value the forms and logic of writing over the forms and logic of speaking. They represent a kind of technology which is homologous with other technologies in our society. Writing also represents permanence and control rather than the impermanence and flux of speech. For these and other reasons writing is the medium of the domain of public social and political life while speaking is the medium of the domain of private life. The 'public person' has to adopt the modes of writing in speaking. For the powerful therefore, there is effectively only the one mode, that of writing; both in writing and in speech. (There are exceptions, such as, in Australia, the figure of the former Premier of Queensland, Sir Bjelke-Petersen. However his mode of public speaking reflects a populism which is accounted for by this theory also. It represents the studied inversion of the norm, with quite clear political reasons and effects.) As a consequence the distinction of private and public has ceased to be relevant in most areas of their lives or rather, the domain of the public extends into areas regarded as essentially private by other members of society.

From what I have said so far it seems clear that mastery of speech, and of writing, confers power and effectiveness in different areas, in differing ways, in different domains. Command of writing gives access to certain cognitive, conceptual, social and political arenas. The person who commands both the forms of writing and of speech is therefore constructed in a fundamentally different way from the person who commands the forms of speech alone. Her or his range of cognitive, conceptual, social and political potential for being and acting differs fundamentally from that of the person who is confined to the forms of speech alone. Participation in public life and the power which that distributes depend on access to and mastery of the forms of writing. The possibility of being a certain kind of speaking and writing subject and therefore a certain kind of social and cultural agent depends on a person's position in and relation to the forms and potentials of speech and of writing.

Command of writing gives access to cognitive, conceptual, social and political arenas.

46

Authors, writers and originality

The general point of my discussion is to demonstrate the effect of social factors on the formation of a text. Discourse and genre both pre-exist the actions of the individual writer; so do the effects of the modes of speech and writing. Indeed, as I have attempted to show, writers are formed **within** discourse, genre, and the possibilities offered by speech and writing. What then is the role of the writer? And what are the demands for originality which can legitimately be made of child writers, or indeed of any writer? Notice that I have not included **speakers** here. It seems that we do not expect speakers to be original or creative in relation to the texts in which they are involved. Rather we seem to take it as assumed that speakers are largely obeying the demands of the occasion—of genre, of discourse, and of speech—when they speak. This may be due to the fact that spoken texts characteristically are multi-speaker texts, so that no one speaker can be given responsibility for the construction of the text. Moreover, in a multi-speaker text the speakers are not only fulfilling the demands of genre and discourse, but also seem to be under the reciprocal influence of each other as they take their turns in speaking. Written texts by contrast have the outward appearance of being the product of a single writer. However, if my argument is correct, then the function of the writer is not that of a **creator** of text, but of an assembler of text. That is, out of her or his experience of other texts, he or she creates a new text which meets the demands of a particular social occasion. My view stands in a fairly radical opposition to views held implicitly and explicitly in various linguistic or educational theories, which generally speaking regard the writer's activity as one in which he or she draws on the resources of the linguistic system 'as such' (or draws on individual psychological, aesthetic resources) in freshly creating a text which fulfils the writer's intentions or which meets the contingent demands of a particular situation. Such views lead on the one hand to demands for 'originality' and 'creativity' in children's writing, and to tensions about plagiarism on the other hand in judgments made about children's writing and other work.

The task of any writer is first and foremost to understand the demands of generic form, the effects and meanings of discourses, and the forms of language in the written mode. The written texts of child learners everywhere bear the signs of the struggle to meet these demands, and everywhere bear the signs of their achievement in doing so. The 'stories' written by children in primary school show the evidence of a (growing) understanding and mastery of narrative form, of narrative episodic structures, of knowledge of the syntax and the words appropriate to a genre, of formulae and of convention. All too frequently their developing understanding and mastery is classified and dismissed as copying, imitation, plagiarism. Here I wish to give one example only, and let that stand for the problem as it presents itself in all curriculum areas, and at all ages.

My example consists of an extract from a stencilled booklet written by a teacher and distributed to his class; the second part consists of

All writers imitate and plagiarise.

See Kress (1982).

47

the answers written by a 15-year-old boy on questions set by the teacher on his text.

Booklet

Man's part in soil erosion

For centuries, man has mercilessly cleared as much of the native vegetation from the surface of the earth as he could, in order to grow his crops or pasture for his animals. He is only now beginning to realise that he has responsibilities towards the land if he wishes to
5   keep it producing for him.

Soil creep

If soil particles lie on a sloping surface, they will tend to move downhill. This effect is called 'soil creep' and is evident on sloping land by the presence of shallow, parallel 'steps'. Normally, the trees
10   and bushes growing on the slope would limit the amount of soil creep on a hillside, but if the land has been cleared, mass movement of topsoil can result. This can be aggravated by stock using the 'steps' continually as paths. Usually, the effects of soil creep take place very slowly, and cannot be seen, but sometimes it is made obvious where
15   fence-posts and trees are seen to lean downhill.
      Prolonged wet weather will saturate the surface soil and 'lubricate' layers of clay which lie beneath the surface of some soils. A section of the surface soil may then move rapidly downhill, causing a landslide.

Answers

Man's part in soil erosion

1. Soil creep is when soil particles on a slope move downhill. 2. Evidence of soil creep is the presence of shallow, parallel 'step'. Also fence post trees tend to lean downhill. 3. The absence of trees and bushes and stock using the 'steps' as pathways aggravates soil creep.
5   Also the same as in number 4. 4. Prolonged wet weather will saturate the surface soil and 'lubricate' layers of clay which lie beneath the surface of some soils. This makes a landslide. 5. We can excuse the early settlers because they weren't used to the climate of Australia and didn't realise the damage they were doing.

I wish to focus on a few features only. Clearly the child writer has mastered the syntax of writing, and much of the syntax of the generic form. His learning here is particularly about the technical terms used in the discipline of geology, and about the use of metaphor as a common strategy in theoretical/scientific writing. Some of the technical terms are highlighted by the teacher by the use of scare-quotes. These are reproduced by the child, in one case without the scare-quotes, in two cases with them. There is therefore straightforward copying, and it is difficult to see what else the child writer could do. He also copies other terms: *soil particles, aggravates, saturate, surface soil, layers of clay*. If we compare, for instance, his third answer with the original text, we can see the relation between model and resultant text clearly: *3. The absence of trees and bushes and stock using the 'steps' as pathways aggravates soil creep.* His answer is a summary of lines 7—13 of the model text. There is an example of direct copying of a whole sentence in the child's fourth answer. Yet while there is direct copying, there is also a significant assimilation and reordering of material. That reordering is itself guided by generic and discursive models, and by the model of written syntax. The writer departs from the model text by not using the passive form of the verb in his third answer. He seems, too, to recognise the use of metaphor involved in 'steps' and 'lubricate' by reproducing these with the quotation marks.

Frequently writers in school are asked to 'state, in your own words . . . .'. My point is that no writers have their 'own words'. Writers have the words—and more importantly, the systematic organisation of words—given to them by the discourses and genres of which they have had experience. The writer is therefore not the creator of 'own words', but the producer of texts. All texts are motivated by difference. The writer's task is to construct a text in which that difference is resolved in a particular way, by constructing a reading position from the point of which that difference is neutralised in a plausible, 'natural' reading. The function of the writer is therefore both a linguistic one—the construction of texts, and a political one—the resolution of difference. The materials available to the writer in carrying out that function are all those texts which have a relationship of relevance to the particular text which is now to be constructed. Every text contracts such relations of INTER-TEXTUALITY with a vast network of other texts. Within and out of that network of relations the writer constructs a new text which everywhere bears the marks of its inter-textual relationships and which is also set off from all those texts, in a relation of CONTRA-TEXTUALITY (to use a term coined by J.R. Martin). This marks the task, the function and the achievement of the writer: the creation of a new text, which while it is entirely constructed in the conventions of genre, of discourse, of writing, of inter-textuality, is also new in being the text appropriate to and arising out of one specific social occasion.

J.R. Martin is the author of *Factual Writing: Exploring and Challenging Social Reality* (1989).

The notion of the writer's 'own words' encapsulates an ambiguity between ownership/possession on the one hand and creation /origination on the other. That distinction is mirrored by the distinction that is drawn in our culture between the concept of the author and that of the writer. Authors are above all writers who own their texts, in the sense of a legal ownership as enshrined in copyright laws. Authors are the producers of material commodities which are treated as the author's property, in a legal and economic sense. Authors do therefore 'speak in their own words' in a legal and economic sense. The texts of an author are entirely identified with the author, in the sense that they are his or her 'issue'; and it is this identification which conveys the status of ownership and property on them. Authors produce not single texts but 'a body of work', and no scribble left by an author escapes scrutiny and evaluation. Every action of an author has significance, so that their garbage cans may be searched by 'readers' for traces of significance. Given this notion of authorship—both an identification of text and author, and a separation of author and 'body of work'—the texts of an author have a social valuation which transcends time. Authors therefore always speak in the 'universal present tense' : 'As Shakespeare

Authors are different from writers; they are writers who literally and legally own their own texts.

49

says in King Lear . . .', 'As Einstein points out . . .'. That is a valuation not accorded to a 'writer', let alone to a 'speaker'.

There is a significant literature dealing with the western notion of the 'author'. See Barthes (1977) and Foucault (1977).

Clearly this notion of author is a social and cultural construct. In many cultures there is no such concept, nor is there any notion that compares with our view of certain texts as commodity and property. The economic function of the author depends on the notion of text as property, which in its turn seems to depend on the prior existence of writing, so that texts can assume a permanent, tangible, material form. The political function of the author derives from and depends on the role he or she performs (or can perform, potentially) in relation to discursive difference, the author's role in legitimating certain discourses, and in constructing relatively permanent reading positions and, therefore, modes of reading and reading formations.

Education aims to produce writers.

My point here is to draw attention to the need to distinguish between the two roles of author and of writer. It seems to me a legitimate and indeed necessary aim of the education system to attempt to produce competent, effective writers. It seems not to be the stated, overt aim of the eduation system to produce authors. Yet in so many instances the demands made of children, and the expectations held of them, are about authorship, rather than about writership. That confusion holds the potential for much harm.

Language and language users

Language users do not have access to 'language as such', to the whole language system abstractly. Their experience of language is mediated through their experiences of texts on social occasions, their knowledge of the systematic organisation of linguistic form through discourses and genres. No language user has experience of all social occasions and of all genres, hence his or her knowledge of language is a particular and a partial one. It matters therefore which texts and what range of texts a language user has had experience of, for that defines his or her stance within and towards the potential of language. The discourses of which she or he has knowledge provide the range of possible subject positions that she or he may assume; similarly with the range of genres. Both together provide the linguistic resources which individual speakers have at their disposal. The resources of a language are therefore arranged around speakers/writers in specific ways, and they can marshall a certain range of linguistic resources. Language therefore has 'a different look' to different speakers/writers. The notion that the resources of language are freely available to any individual is as potent as the notion that the material benefits of the capitalist system are freely available to all; and as misleading. There is of course no barrier to anyone becoming a successful capitalist—indeed the ideological strength of the system depends on that, though as it happens the structures of most of our lives tend to make it unlikely. Similarly with language. Anyone can get access to any of the resources of language; but as with material acquisitions so with linguistic potential: the social structures in which we find ourselves make it difficult and unlikely.

No one comes 'freshly' to language. Through the social place we occupy, language meets us already organised in certain ways, in certain sets of discourses, genres, in spoken or written modes. Hence children grow up in contexts in which certain texts, discourses, genres, the modes of speech or writing, already have certain configurations. These are the forms which become habitual, and once habitual become 'natural' for a child growing into society and into language. And these initial configurations have a strong determining effect through the range of discourses and genres which structure the texts, in providing subject positions, assigning reading positions, roles of dominance or subordination within specific discourses and genres, facilitating or impeding modes of thinking and modes of acting, giving prominence to modes of the public or of the private domain in the forms of speech and writing.

All these matters, which are in one sense no more nor less than habitual uses, nevertheless are in another sense those modes and forms which are known, comfortable and congenial, natural, which can and do become 'language as such' for the individual language user. Again it is necessary to stress that by 'individual' I do not mean 'non-social'. It is social structures and processes which lead to that set of circumstances, though from the individual's point of view the circumstances seem not social but natural, and her or his situation seems and is entirely individual.

When a child comes to school, many of these factors have already had a long-lasting effect. Despite myths to the contrary—romantic myths of the innocence of childhood—children have already assumed subject positions; have acquired certain degrees of power as language users—or not as the case may be; may be in tune with the discourses of the school or may find themselves in a clash with them. These are matters to which teachers, curriculum designers, and educational philosophers need to attend, for they are the foundations on which educational success and failure equally are founded.

Chapter 3

Power and language

Keeping one's distance

Power is about relations of difference, whether it is the relationship between the weightlifter and 250kg of steelbar, the relationship between muscleman and the 9-stone weakling with sand in his eyes, or the relations of power which are the effects of difference in social structures. It is these latter that I wish to talk about here. Because of the constant unity of language and other social matters, language is entwined in social power in a number of ways: it indexes power, expresses power, and language is involved wherever there is contention over and challenge to power. Power does not derive from language, but language may be used to challenge power, to subvert it, and to alter distributions of power in the short or in the longer term.

The metaphor which best describes effects of power is that of space and distance. Imagine the court of some oriental potentate. Degrees of power difference between the ruler and the courtiers, supplicants, emissaries and servants, are precisely indicated by each person's distance from the throne, and their posture—whether upright facing the ruler, lying face-down at some distance, or backing away from the throne in a permanent bow. Space is still a well-understood indicator of power—the size of a house, garden, office, car, swimming-pool, desk— can all indicate power. So do spatial arrangements in classrooms, offices, waiting-rooms, public buildings and spaces.

Indeed, space may come close to being a biologically determined signifier—animals which live in 'social' groups indicate power by space and posture. It seems that where physical space is limited, the physical category of spatial distance is rotated through ninety degrees, so to speak, and becomes the abstract distance of social hierarchy. The pecking order of chickens contains aspects of both systems.

Language provides the most finely articulated means for a nuanced registration of differences in power in social hierarchical structures, both as a static system and in process. All linguistic forms which can be used to indicate relations of distance, and those which can indicate 'state' or 'process' serve the expression of power. In fact there are few linguistic forms which are not pressed into the service of the expression of power, by a process of syntactic/textual metaphor. Interviews are social occasions and genres which are about differences of power, among other things. Here I will briefly analyse an interview text to consider some of the indicators of distance and of power.

Interview text

	Max	A couple of questions very easy to answer for a radio program we're doing the first of the questions is: **What** would you say language is?
5	Woman	Language . . . well it's the dialogue that people speak within various countries.
	Max	Fair enough aaand **what** would you say it's made **out** of?
	Woman	[8 second pause]. It's made out of [puzzling intonation]
	Max	Hmmm
10	Woman	Well I don't know how you'd tell what it's **made** out of it's a person's **expression** I suppose is it?
	Max	I haven't got the answers I've only got the questions [laughing]
	Woman	[simultaneously—small laugh]
15	Sid	That's not **bad** though
	Woman	Well it's an **expression** it would be a person's expression wouldn't it?
	Sid	That's a good answer
	Max	Thank you very much

Distance is being expressed by both interviewer and interviewee. The interviewer's initial question **What** *would you say* is distanced in a number of ways. It is a command, which, in a different genre, where the interviewer had relatively greater power (a lesson, say), might have been expressed as an imperative 'Tell me what . . .'. The choice of interrogative rather than imperative indicates a shift from an assertion of power to a modulation of it 'I'm only asking . . .' rather than 'I'm telling you to . . .'. The use of the modal auxiliary *would* within the question is another distancing device, making the asking of the question a hypothetical possibility 'If I were to ask you, what would you say . . .', as though it had not been or was not going to be asked. Notice too the difference in the interviewer's introduction to the question here, and in the interview with Max and John (and Sid) in Chapter 1. In the interview under discussion, Max said: *for a radio program we're doing.* *I* and *we* indicate different stances by the interviewer (I am not here interested in the question of 'truth') towards the interviewee. *We* disperses responsibility, includes the speaker in a larger (how large?) group, gives some anonymity and impersonality. *We* could be the *we* of an institution. It, too, therefore acts as a distancing device.

Who in this genre is the relatively more powerful participant? The less powerful participant, the interviewee also uses distancing strategies. For instance, she uses 'tag questions': line 11 *I suppose is it?*; and line 17 *wouldn't it?*. This tag question solicits support from the other participant, and thereby downgrades the answer from the status of 'information' to the status of 'request for support' or 'tentative inquiry'. The use of *I suppose* has a modal force, giving the clauses which are subordinated to it (*it's a person's expression I suppose*) the status of 'supposition' rather than of fact. Placing the main clause *I suppose* after its subordinate clause further diminishes the force of the statement—it is both syntactically dominated and concluded by the modality of supposition.

The woman's *how you'd tell* ('how would you tell?') encapsulates that meaning. She attributes the possibility of the answer and the knowledge to her questioner. The interviewee uses the modal auxiliary *would* in the way the interviewer does : line 10 *Well I don't know how you'd tell what it's made out of*; line 16 *Well it's an expression it would be a person's expression wouldn't it?* This last instance is particularly revealing, for here the speaker changes from the verb *to be* in the universal present tense, expressing a modality of certainty, to the hypothetical/conditional *would be*, expressing a modality of tentativeness.

The mode of distancing the woman interviewee chooses to use is through the ostensive content. By that I mean that the speaker attaches a modality of uncertainty to her statements, to the information that they are providing: 'I'm venturing this as an opinion, not as fact, I can't be certain about it.' This might be because she is uncertain, or it might be because in the face of the other participant's power (however perceived) she would rather not commit herself too firmly to any point of view. If the other participant then chooses to challenge that view (thereby challenging the speaker) there is always the option of stepping back from any commitment to that view 'I only said it might', 'I was only giving an opinion'. In other words, what operates here is an inverse relation of power and knowledge: in the face of superior power the status of her knowledge becomes inferior. This can be easily established in this example by some of the points I have already discussed. For instance, the shift by the interviewee from certainty to tentativeness in line 16 *Well, it's an expression it would be a person's expression.*

Clearly it is possible for this woman to be certain, as she is and remains in line 4 *Language . . . well it's the dialogue.* It is not lack of knowledge but lack of power which introduces the uncertainty. In this interview, Sid uses the modality of certainty (i.e. the so-called universal present) *That's not bad though, That's a good answer*, where he could have said 'You could be/might be right'.

Max too uses the present tense for that purpose *a radio program we're doing* (rather than 'a radio program we'd like to do'); or *I haven't got the answers* rather than 'I wouldn't like to say'. Max uses the modal auxiliary *would* to indicate tentativeness. However he distances himself not through the content but through (or about) the interaction *What would you say language is?* i.e. 'If I were to ask you—and that's what I'm tentative about—then what would be your response?' Max casts doubt on the possibility of the interaction; the woman casts doubt on the status of her knowledge. These two strategies have very different psychological and social consequences.

Comparing the woman's responses with those of Sid in the interview discussed in Chapter 1 makes this point even more clearly: Sid's views are all couched in the modality of certainty: *Language is communication between.* No tentative tag questions seeking support here, no modal auxiliaries signalling tentativeness. For some reason, in the

54

same type of interaction, Sid values his knowledge differently, more highly, with greater certainty than the woman does. I shall discuss the reason in the next section; though clearly it has to do with the distribution of power.

It might be worth drawing out one implication of this situation for the education process generally, both for teachers and for learners. The first point concerns the close interconnection, and at times identity, of power and knowledge. The statements of the powerful can count as knowledge by virtue of their power. This has important consequences for teaching strategies, for the way in which the interrelation of teachers and learners is structured. In some situations the hidden curriculum may revolve around this question 'How is knowledge defined, by what processes is knowledge established as knowledge?' If students are taught, by virtue of the structures and processes of pedagogic interaction, not to value or to undervalue their knowledge, then that has consequences for how teachers see students, and for how students come to see themselves.

Of course we need to recognise that outside of this particular situation the woman interviewee is likely to value her knowledge quite differently. Talking with friends, she might well say '. . . it's a person's expression, that's what it is!' without tag questions and without tentative modalities. And similarly with children outside of school, where they value their own knowledge at whatever the going rate is in their particular peer group. The important points about this are: In how many situations is any one speaker's knowledge valued by himself or herself and by the other participants? What kinds of situations are they, what is their social valuation? Does the speaker operate more often in situations in which her or his knowledge is always undervalued? For instance, are there institutionalised distributions of power such that the young, the female, the very old, the non-whites, the workers or the unemployed tend to be more frequently in situations where their knowledge is not valued, than do the adult, the male, the white, the bosses and managers?

To conclude this section I want to discuss a question raised and left by my analysis of the interview. The interviewer and the interviewee **both** use distancing forms. If the interviewer is more powerful, why should he do so? As in all of my account, there are a number of answers. The interviewer **is** the more powerful participant here, he does control the interview entirely. As the more powerful participant, he has the option of asserting his power or disguising it **somewhat**. He chooses to disguise it, somewhat. For instance, he is much more in control here than in the interview with John and Sid; this interview never threatens to become a conversation. Generally speaking—and this 'generally' needs much and constant qualification—in Anglo-Saxon middle-class social groups in Australia (as in Britain) there is a 'politeness' convention which suggests that the powerful should not normally openly assert their power. This is a situation where this convention obtains. The participants are middle class; the interviewer is a male academic, the interviewee a well-dressed woman, well beyond middle age. The appearance of the woman suggests that she is of the interviewer's social class, hence there is a kind of solidarity. Her age is such that it commands 'respect'— that is, she is not of an age which elicits condescension, and both interviewer and interviewee are of a generation which is familiar with the convention of 'respect to one's elders'. The fact that the interaction is conducted across a gender division adds a distancing factor.

That is one answer. Another answer is that the interviewer's language contains nowhere near as many indicators of tentativeness as does the interviewee's. And, as I have pointed out, their distancing occurs in a significantly different manner; the interviewee's through and about content; the interviewer's through and about the interaction. His greater power is intact. A further answer is that the two participants have quite different aims; and each uses language to achieve those aims. The interviewer needs a favour; the interviewee is faced, out of the blue, with a perplexing situation in which she has to work out on the spot what this is actually about. It is entirely understandable that she waves a kind of verbal umbrella to keep this assailant at arm's length.

Language, gender, and power

It remains to be explained why the woman interviewee values her knowledge less highly, why her language shows so many more signs of tentativeness, than that of the male interviewees in the interview in Chapter 1, in the same situation. My response is that she has, in this interaction, both a different reading position and a different subject position from that of the interviewer. The male interviewees have the same subject position as the interviewer, and are attempting, not necessarily consciously, to subvert the reading position constructed for them in the interview. Although the situations are largely similar, there are significant differences. Max knew Sid and John, who were responsible for the repair of his car; all are male, of very similar age; both Sid and John for their part and Max for his might think of themselves as being of a different class. Max did not know the woman interviewee; interviewer and interviewee were of a significantly different age-group, and interacted across the gender divide. Interviewer and interviewee might have thought of themselves as being of the same class.

Given this situation I suggest that the men construct the woman interviewee within sexist (and ageist) discourse, that she allows herself to be constructed like that for the duration of the interview, or perhaps that she has permanently adopted the subject position of 'elderly woman' as constructed in sexist discourse. There is the evidence of her own use of language—neither Sid nor John use tag questions, or the modal auxiliary of hypothetical possibility. That suggests that the men adopt the subject position constructed for **them** in sexist discourse—assertive, confident, blunt—and the woman does too. There is also the evidence of the difference in the interaction: Sid and John constantly challenge Max's control of the interview, disregarding his controlling instructions. For instance Max's closing *Terrific thanks a lot* is quite ignored by John who continues as though Max had not spoken : *I don't know*. Similarly with Max's second closing. Sid enters the interview unbidden, and has 'the last word'.

Control of the social occasion, of the genre of the text, is a sign of power: here that power is constantly challenged. The woman interviewee on the other hand acquiesces totally in the interviewer's control. The interviewer's closings (which also act as valuations/acceptances of the responses) differ. With Sid and John: *Terrific thanks a lot, that's wonderful thanks a lot*; with the woman: *Fair enough, thank you very much*. It is left to the uninvited Sid to provide valuations *That's not **bad** though* and *That's a good answer*. In the interview with John he makes no attempt at all at valuation. Sid may (unconsciously) see his actions as a gentlemanly support of an elderly lady; which would confirm my analysis.

It is no coincidence that Sid and John are not reluctant to challenge the interviewer's power. The subject position of adult male, of working-class male perhaps, encourages that mode of action—not in general, but in a situation such as this. In a different situation, perhaps where Max might be interviewing Sid for admission to a tertiary course as a mature-age student, the interrelation would be altered significantly enough for such a challenge to be prohibited. Max would there assume the subject position of male professional (constructed in sexist and in professional discourse), rather than here where he is male client.

The retreat into impersonality and mystification

The distancing strategies adopted by all the participants in the two interviews involved a certain stance towards the content of the interaction, or to the possibility of an interaction. However, all participants remain visible (or audible) as individual persons. The source of power is to that extent obvious, and therefore potentially open to challenge. The powerful individual may however choose to exercise power invisibly (inaudibly) by retreating as an individual. There are a number of strategies available and here I will discuss some prominent ones. Generally the strategies are of two kinds: a retreat into an institutional impersonality, or a retreat into individual invisibility. The effect in each case is to make the sources of power or authority difficult to detect, and therefore difficult or impossible to challenge.

In the previous two chapters I discussed one example of impersonal texts, namely those of science, as they appear in school textbooks. I said that the ideology of science insists on impersonality as an indicator of 'objectivity': the individual investigator is irrelevant, indeed the intrusion of her or his 'subjectivity' would be a subversion of the ideology. This lends objectivity, and therefore the appearance of immutable truth and factuality to the statements of science. It also endows the statements made by the institution of science, through individual scientists, with great power. That power can be and is used by individual scientists, for every ideology has its inversion. One aspect of scientific activity is that certain individuals are given and exercise great power, derived from the ideology of science.

Much institutional language operates quite similarly to that of science. Individual subjects are absent, and with them the processes performed by individuals, in **time**. Instead there are abstractions, states rather than processes; the syntax is nominal rather than verbal, the texts are overtly, outwardly monologic rather than dialogic, the tenses are timeless, such processes as there are, are about relations and definitions; abstract entities seem to act independently of human causation. Here, to make my point concrete is a brief example. (The full text will be discussed at length in Chapter 4.)

Letter

With any innovation it is expected that the motive is to meet more effectively the needs of students. A sound reason for rejecting, say, a trial of 'setting' English or Mathematics or indeed of classes in any given subject, might be that there were insufficient teachers of the appropriate
5   kind available at the one time to organise it. An unsound reason would be that 'setting' is perhaps more difficult to arrange administratively.

No experiment must commit the Education Department to supply more staff, more accommodation, more equipment or more funds without prior consultation. Nor must parents be put to expense without
10   their concurrence.

The question of government in a school is of prime importance, and should therefore make provision, especially in secondary schools, for student opinion to make itself known. Ways of bringing this about will differ with the size and nature of each school, and the relative age and
15   maturity of the student concerned. Methods are best left for the schools to work out.

Finally, the sooner the old concept of the fixed timetable and strictly regulated movement as the blueprint of the school day disappears, the better.
20   The timetable should reflect a great variety of individual approaches. The timetable should be the servant of the curriculum, and both be servants to the student.

A large number of the syntactic forms have missing subject/agents, that is, the speaking subject, the source of the utterance, or of the power, or of authority is not given, nor readily recoverable. Agentless passives are one such form: *it is expected, be put, to make itself known, the fixed timetable . . . regulated movement*. Similarly with the non-finite form *to meet more effectively, to organise it, to arrange, to work out*. Here too the speaking/acting subject is missing; we know that there is one, and we may guess about it, but we cannot be certain about his/her/their identity. Another non-finite form has the same effect: *reason for rejecting, a trial of 'setting' English*. Nouns which stand in a determinable relation to full clauses—nominalisations—belong here too, from that point of view. So *any innovation it is* (where *innovation* is related to 'someone innovates'), No *experiment* ('someone experiments'), *without prior consultation* ('someone consults' with someone else), *The question of government, provision*. The point about all these forms is that discernible beyond them are verbal process form, in which agents, speaking subjects, causes, are at work and exist. The fact that clauses which reported concrete actions in time have been transformed by the writer into abstract entities or concepts out of time, makes the text not only impersonal, which it has literally become, but also mystifies all those processes and their participants. We know that something was/is going on beyond the surface; but we cannot discover what. The

58

use of a noun such as *motive* without any indication of **whose** motive has a similar effect.

Prohibitions and injunctions are stated in various parts of this extract, without the source of the prohibition or of the injunction being revealed: *No experiment must commit, Nor must parents be put, The timetable should reflect.* Judgments are made and possibilities advanced without any indication of their source: *A sound reason . . . might be, An unsound reason would be.* Definitional statements in the form of 'X is Y' abound, again without any indication of the origins of the definition : *the motive is to meet, The question . . . is of prime importance, Methods are best left.* The use of the universal present tense, giving the modal force of certainty, gives the definitions the effect of immutable laws.

The overall effect is that of a world of abstract entities and relations, frozen in time, objectified processes, a kind of verbal Marie Celeste, left intact but without any human agents. In fact what agency there is has become transferred to abstract entities and inanimate objects, so that schools work out methods, questions make provisions, opinions make themselves known, innovations have motives, experiments threaten to commit Education Departments, timetables and regulated movements spontaneously disappear, the timetable is the servant of the master curriculum, and both are servants to the (singular) student.

Power here lies with the writer whose relation to the institution is somewhat ambiguous: does he use the impersonality of institutional forms to achieve his aims, or is he in fact the tool of the institution and of its discourses, a scribe merely, written by discourse and genre to produce a text which will control its readers? (In writing in this fashion I am myself using forms and strategies quite like the ones I have been analysing.) The text does exert power, through its appeals to a vague, but not ineffective authority, its immutable definitions, its timeless statements.

Bureaucratic language is so offensive because it is so far removed from that fundamental form of language and social interaction, the dialogue. Or at least, on the surface it has no dialogic features, no flux, no process but only control and rigidity. There are many stages of this process, ranging from the occasional use of such features even in casual informal spoken texts, to the totally impersonal 'No Parking' sign. Here everything has been reduced, there is only the noun and its negation: no one speaks, writes, no one is constructed as reader, the sign's message exists out of time in all time, unchallengeable and beyond dialogue except by the physical action of defacement, destruction.

To the extent that speech and spoken interaction are always open to challenge, to irruptions and subversions, bureaucratic language has the advantage of preventing any such opportunity: it provides no spaces for that. Where control is wanted, the relatively open forms of speech genres are too risky.

So far I have mentioned several strategies for achieving an expression of power difference. Speakers may remain visible or become invisible, may choose to effect distancing by modulating the content of their texts ('it would be a person's') or by focusing on some aspect of their interpersonal relation with an audience ('what would you say').

Invisibility, impersonality may take the form of a retreat into an institutional voice, into the language of bureaucracy, or it may involve the refusal of the speaker to identify herself or himself. One instance of that was Max's shift from *I* to *we* between the two interviews. A most common form of this occurs in the everyday practice of 'naming'. In Max's case he had the choice of naming himself as the individual *I* or as part of a group *we*. There are other choices he could have made, 'I'm interviewing for a radio program' naming himself in his role of interviewer; 'Excuse me, I'm doing this for 2SER-FM', naming himself as worker/employee; or 'Would you be interested in helping us at 2SER-FM', 'I'm from 2SER-FM', naming himself by the institution. Each form indicates certain relations of distance or of proximity, and of power.

See Brown & Gilman (1960).

The pronouns of power are also discussed by Cate Poynton in *Language and Gender: Making the Difference* (1989).

In an immensely fruitful article 'The pronouns of power and solidarity' Brown and Gilman traced the development of pronoun use in several European languages. They focused on the distinction, still present in modern French, German, and Italian, among European languages (similar and frequently much more complex systems exist in, for instance, Asian languages) between the uses of *tu* and *vous*, *Sie* and *du*, a distinction which still operated in the English of Shakespeare's day in the *thou* (singular) and *you* (plural distinction). Briefly, the plural pronoun was (is) used towards the more powerful person, who would (could) return the singular form. People willing to affirm 'solidarity' would use the singular form to each other. The plural form therefore signalled power, the singular form powerlessness, or solidarity. In all of Shakespeare's plays, the use of singular and plural pronouns is a precise indicator of fluctuating relations of power. At the opening of *King Lear*, for instance, the two Earls of Gloucester and Kent are in conversation: Kent uses the singular pronoun *I*, Gloucester the plural *we/us*—until his bastard son Edmund appears on the stage, and he explains to Kent how there was 'good sport' at Edmund's making, with his saucy mother. Brown and Gilman assume that the success of the powerful *you* over the powerless or intimate *thou* is a sign of the increasing democratisation of English society, that is, a society in which power difference and superiority could no longer be openly asserted. My analysis shows rather that while power indications have gone from this particular instance (but do still exist in differences of *I*, *we*), they are spread everywhere else in the linguistic system, at every point. Democratisation seems therefore to be a myth.

Or perhaps a more adequate account is that if the expression of power in one particular form comes under sustained challenge, the place and use of that form on social occasions in discourses, in genres and in text diminishes and disappears. In language there are a very large number of other forms which can be pressed into service of the same feature. The question is whether it is the challenge to power that succeeds or whether it is the challenge to a particular form of its expression that succeeds. In the case of English, the expression of power through the *you/thou* distinction has disappeared, but continues everywhere else in discourses, genres and texts. In French and German the expression of power through the *du/Sie*, *tu/vous* distinction has been and is still under challenge, but has not yet disappeared. Speakers of French and German learning and speaking English are most sensitive to the apparent democraticness of the English forms, and are struck equally by what they come to regard as its disguised assertions of power in the forms that I have discussed.

Classification, valuation and metaphor

Names bring actions into consciousness and into the domain of social life. Actions without names are not social—they cannot be brought within spoken or unspoken laws, and hence can be neither prohibited nor encouraged, condoned or ignored. Such actions do of course exist— but they remain in the domain for which we use names such as 'feeling', 'emotion', 'intuition', and so on. A name, once in existence, exerts power and can be used to exert power. In the mid to late 1950s, cross-gender sexual relations were regulated by, among others, terms such as 'dating', 'going steady', 'necking', 'petting' (of which there were two varieties in my vocabulary, 'light petting' and 'heavy petting'). These terms acted to control modes of behaviour for a certain social group in finely nuanced ways, with permissions, prohibitions and penalties. As a young 'New Australian' becoming socialised into a new culture, I encountered that area of social life first through the names, learned modes of behaviour and modes of being and thinking before I encountered the social practices. That direction of learning is not at all unusual, the linguistic preceding the other social modes. That has given rise to a quite powerful view, namely that the social world is constructed by language, that language has created the social world.

In my view, that is not the case. 'Petting' did not become a social practice with the invention of the word: rather, a complex of changes in society, of which the linguistic was just one, brought about certain changes in the possibilities of modes of sexual behaviour among adolescents. Once established, the linguistic forms seem to exert power autonomously; and indeed, as one of many other social practices, linguistic practice does have social effects.

The ability to create new names, new categories, is therefore one with powerful consequences. The kind of new names that I have in mind are not the once-off coinages, but those names/words created out of existing linguistic resources, using linguistic processes governed by the demands of discourse and genre. It is an activity of creation which is performed by individuals in the social manner of all linguistic activity. The text below contains several instances. The occasion was one where a group of parents had formed a 'Waterbabies' swimming club, and one member of the group had been given the job of writing a set of rules for the new club.

For a detailed discussion of this text, see Fowler, Hodge, Kress & Trew (1979).

Club rules

1 Parents must accompany and take responsibility for their children at all times, unless the child is in the water in an instructed class.
 Note—In most cases this will mean one adult enrolling with one child, or, if they so wish, one adult with more than one child provided it is understood they are responsible for them.

2 Being absent for more than three consecutive sessions without explanation to the membership secretary means automatic expulsion.
3 No outside shoes will be worn when in the pool area.
4 Please respect the facilities and equipment, and take particular care with untrained children.
5 The age limits of the club are six months to eight years. For the six to eight years old instruction will be provided. Children may remain members for the completed term in which their eighth birthday falls.
6 There must be no more than 24 bodies in the pool at any one time.
7 Membership cards must always be carried and shown on request.

This is a text arising in a situation where modes of action have to be newly defined, where a new social world is to be created. It is also one where the new text is constrained by a knowledge of and the demands made by an existing genre, that of (club) rules, and constrained by existing discourses of authority. There are a number of categories newly coined in this text, for this situation. *Outside shoes* in rule 3 is one such category. Its effect is to give the category of 'shoes' a new valuation. Clearly, if there are 'outside shoes' there must be 'inside shoes', perhaps 'pool-side shoes', 'fireside shoes', 'bedroom shoes', and others. What the term does is to force readers to think that there might be a whole classificatory area of which they are ignorant but to which they need to attend. *Instructed class* in rule 1 acts similarly; it immediately calls up the negative form 'uninstructed class'. It forces parents to think about their children in new terms, as 'instructed' or 'uninstructed', 'partially instructed' or 'well instructed', 'under-' or 'overinstructed'. Rule 4 introduces the term *untrained children*; again the creation of this term calls into being a whole set of categories around the term 'nearly trained', 'fully trained', etc.

The rules do assist in bringing a new social world into being, and anyone who wishes to be a member of that world will have to know and abide by its potent namings. Not only will members have to think differently about their shoes, in ways which had not perhaps occurred or mattered to them before; as parents they will have to think about their children, using quite new terms of relevance, terms which previously did not exist and which here and now have primary relevance.

In this, the parents' concern for and attitude towards their children is being refocused; children assume a different relevance in a new system of valuation. There is a process of classification at work here, which repositions the parents' notion of their children—and the children themselves—in a new classificatory system. We may wish to think about this new system as being simply an extension of the former system, by an addition of a new set of relevant criteria ('trainedness', 'instructedness'); or we may think of the addition as effecting a reconstitution, a re-ordering of the whole system. That is, a way of thinking about children which includes 'trainedness', 'instructedness', brings about a quantitative change to the whole system, in which all the other criteria of relevance are affected. For instance, 'behavedness' may lose some importance in the face of 'trainedness' or 'instructedness': a parent may cease to attribute so much relevance to a child being well behaved if she or he proves to be 'badly instructed'.

If I seem to be labouring this point it is because it is enormously important in all of social life, and in education particularly. The education process is about the processes of classification, repositioning individuals with respect to potent social/cultural classificatory systems, re-ordering the classificatory systems of those who are the learners. Power is involved at every point in that process, in the struggle over particular terms, over whose classificatory systems are to prevail, whose are to be valued and whose are to be dismissed. Within each discipline and across the whole curriculum there are struggles over classification. In the process the learner discovers categories of culturally relevant and valued knowledge, and also discovers the significance of power in the construction of knowledge. In school—as on certain other social occasions and in certain other structures—the powerful can and do enforce their classifications as 'knowledge'. This may happen on the most trivial instances, using the most minute linguistic forms, or it may happen on highly-charged occasions, involving language at the highest level. As an instance of the former, consider the very frequent case of an alternative pronunciation that occurs in a conversation. A committee chairperson might say 'advertisement', placing stress on the third syllable, with the vowel pronounced as in 'high'. If the term continues to be used, committee members then have the choice of continuing that pronunciation, or pronouncing it 'correctly'. If the chairperson is considerably more powerful than the members, the decision to pronounce the word 'correctly' will be felt by all as a challenge to the chairperson. If a member does not wish to compromise, an alternative strategy will be to avoid using that term, thus neither compromising principle nor issuing a challenge. Even though it seems somewhat remote, 'distance' and 'distancing' are involved in this example. Here it is the phonetic distance between one pronunciation and another, and the phonetic distance which either participant potentially needs to move. 'Avoidance', my last-mentioned strategy, of course also involves distance and space. Clearly, such issues, at every level, are the substance of the processes of education. The manner in which they are resolved gives an insight into the principles at work in a given situation.

Before leaving the matter of classification, I wish to discuss the effects of classification at the highest level, the classification of the various forms of language and of languages within one social group. Any social grouping which is not totally homogeneous has differing forms of language available. These may be forms that have developed out of geographical proximity and/or isolation, out of social proximity and distance, they may be class-based languages (the 'high' and 'low' forms of many languages) or gender-based languages (the male and female languages of many social groups, often developed around particular cultural valuations and prohibitions). In a multiracial, multiethnic society such as Australia, these may be entirely distinct languages. In such societies every mature speaker has knowledge of and usually speaking competence in several of these forms. To some extent—and this area like all the others of social activity is closely governed by socially imposed rules—speakers have the possibility of using one rather than another of these forms. At the same time, all these language variants are part of a classificatory system, which places each form in relation to all others in a hierarchy of social/cultural valuation. At the most obvious level we know that 'speaking nicely' is still valued by certain groups of speakers—if not for themselves then certainly for others; speaking (or more often writing) properly is highly valued by a large number of groups, from parents to teachers to employers. In Australia non-English languages tend to have a lower valuation than forms of English, and non-English languages themselves are ranged in complex hierarchies of value, status and power.

In considering this question it is important to bear in mind that value systems are always established from a certain point of view. The point of view which I am adopting here is that of white Anglo-Saxon 'establishment' society. From the point of view of a newly arrived immigrant the system of valuation will be a different one, both taking account of the establishment's system (however well understood) and independent of it. For instance, among German immigrants, the German establishment's system of valuations of German forms is still active, as well as the German system of valuation of other, non-German languages. All of these are subject to specific historical variations depending on when the immigrant left her or his native society, and all of these stand in tension with the system of valuations deriving from the Australian establishment system.

Using one rather than another form therefore becomes a matter subject to the laws of social power much in the way of all other linguistic forms. For instance, using working-class informal, casual speech in a job interview for a particular job has quite specific meanings and quite specific consequences. The relatively less powerful participant may feel pressure to adjust to the language of the more powerful. Persistence with a form of language may signal a challenge to the power of other participants; the continued use of a language form by a number of speakers in the presence of a speaker who is not familiar with or competent in that form may signal exclusion.

The point is worth making particularly in relation to the education system, where this question constantly arises—over matters of class, race, and ethnicity, in a situation where power difference is permanently institutionalised.

This area has been studied extensively within linguistics, under headings such as BILINGUALISM, DIGLOSSIA, CODE SWITCHING. I wish to conclude here by a brief discussion of one such form, that of Aboriginal English. The text is part of a speech delivered by Punch Thompson, a member of the Pitjantjatjara Land Council at Elder Park in Adelaide on 18 May 1980. A colleague of mine, Stephen Muecke, recorded and transcribed this speech:

For a recent, detailed introduction to this area, see Fasold (1984).

Speech

Chairperson : I will now give our first speaker—
and I would like to ask the speakers—
not to draw on—
but jus' get to the point—

64

5 (of) what we're all on about—[applause]
so that thing don't get boring for here—
or they don't get, out of breath or keep repeating
themselves what they're talking about—
an' I happen to be one of these big offenders—
10 How about it Punch Thompson? How about a big hand? [P.T:
Thank YOU] for Punch Thompson [P.T: Thank you] [applause]
of the Pitjantjatjara Land Council [applause]
Thank you very much everyone coming—
um—
15 we want everyone to listen *purkangu*—
that's mean *purka* listen—
be carepul—
um—
we keep waiting people to understand—
20 for relationship—
to the land—
all spirit this is the land—
all mother and father and—
all children—
25 if we lose him—
we lose the land—
we lose the name—
we are trying, pretty hard—
to make—
30 agreement—
the governmen' people, ignorance!—
because they didn' understand—
and some people in city—
they call ignorance—
35 because they didn' understand Aboriginal people—
we living in the land—
that's our land—
we want 'em to listen us—
purka 'cos that's mean 'be carepul' —
40 for their land—
this is our land—
not for European people—
but the South Australian Government—
it didn't understand—
45 we call ignorance—[Yep!]
we want [??] Mr. Donkin—
to be able to give us best bill—
we want the people of South Australia—
to understand, us—
50 *purkangu*—

This example may serve to stand for all others. How are we to
judge this form of English? One dominant mode has been to value it
as a deviant form—however defined, as substandard, deficient,
whatever. Implicit in such a judgment are two assumptions: (1) that

there is one unambiguously, unquestionably defined, established standard and that other forms therefore **are** deviations from it, and (2) that language is autonomous from social structure and occasions of use. The moment we abandon the second assumption, we are forced to value each form of language in relation to the social place with which it is always completely interconnected. Any notion of a 'standard' must then appear as what it is, a socio-political construct, an instrument of power and control by (a) powerful group(s) *vis-à-vis* other groups, less powerful.

When we do see a particular form of language in relation to its social provenance, other questions emerge, questions of the kind I discussed in Chapters 1 and 2, about social, cognitive, and psychological meanings and functions. To do so we need to adopt a constantly critical stance towards our own practices and assumptions, in every detail and at every level. For instance, in the case of the example above, it is essential that the speech was transcribed in the way it was—not as continuous lines, nor as attempted (and therefore failed) sentences; but as a mode of public oratory derived from an entirely different tradition, with meanings entirely related to that tradition. As an example of that here is another brief extract from a longer text, of an Aboriginal narrative told in Aboriginal English. The example comes from *gularabulu*, a collection of stories told by Paddy Roe, told to and edited by Stephen Muecke.

Aboriginal narrative

```
    Yeah we'll talk about this bugawamba you know—
    [Stephen: Yeah bugawamba]
    bugawamba that's the stone we show you—
    all right—
 5  now—
    this is old Duegara—
    you know that's Duegara that's a true man you know—
    he's a true person—
    this time I seen 'im too—
10  old man he's a king—
    Duegara—
    he's a king—
    he had his wife too—
    married tribal way you know—
15  his wife—
    so—
    this 'nother young fella come along he—
    young man come along he pinch his woman—
    you know take 'im away from 'im steal 'im—
20  run away with 'im—
    took 'im 'way—
    he took 'im riight up to—
    Beagle Bay—
    Lombadina—
25  aall round that country he bin round there ooh nearly
    one year I think round that place—
```

and then he—
all these people come back now he thought this old fella
forget about this fella you know, well he had to
30 come back to—
to make himself clear you know—
they must have a fight—
in tribal way—
to make it square whether he can give 'im this—
35 if they have a fight well he can let him have this
woman—
if the old fella beat 'im well—
beat the young fella well old man will have to bring that
woman back—
40 but if the young fella can beat him well he can take the
woman—
it's that way

(P. Roe, *gularabulu*, Fremantle Arts Centre Press, Fremantle, WA, 1982,
pp. 21–2)

The origins of the mode of delivery of the public speech in Aboriginal narrative can now be seen; and its integral relation to, function in, and identity with that culture understood. But to do so it was necessary to challenge a seemingly neutral, value-free practice, such as the transcription of a speech into written form.

Summary: classification as a system of meaning and action

The examples that I have given are in no way an exhaustive survey of either the area of classification, or of its exploitation in the relations of power expressed through language. In Chapter 4 for instance I discuss an area of syntax, namely that of causation and agency, which is yet another highly charged field in this area. My intention here is to bring the importance of the topic into focus, particularly in the context of education, the field of classification and power *par excellence*.

Because my analyses are somewhat discursive and not exhaustive they may give the misleading impression of randomness and casualness. All social activity, linguistic activity included, is always systematic, governed ultimately by larger ideologies. It is only in the discovery and description of the whole system, and its interconnection with other systems, that the meaning of any social activity can be fully understood.

Chapter 4

Values and meaning: the operation of ideology through texts

Ideology and order: taking a position

The contradictions and paradoxes of which so much of social life consists continuously lead to problems which need to find resolution. In Chapter 2, I pointed to the importance of the role of the 'writer' and the role of the 'author' in their task of constructing texts in which conflicts find temporary or permanent resolution. At the same time I suggested that writers and authors already find themselves in certain social/discursive positions which structure their writing to a greater or lesser degree. This apparent contradiction of freedom to construct texts on the one hand and the constraints experienced by a writer in the speaking or writing of a text on the other is explained by the operation of ideologies in a particular culture and society.

Texts provide reading positions for any reader of the text, which the reader may accept or reject, partially or as a whole. These are constructed by the writer of the text. But the writer of the text finds that she or he occupies a writing position with respect to any particular text which guides, influences, determines her or his writing. There is always one or a number of points of view already existent with respect to particular issues. These exist due to the ordering effect of ideologies. To take a simple example from another geography textbook.

Tropical savanna pastoral region
The environmental conditions of this region mean that it is poorly suited to most forms of agriculture. It receives most of its rainfall during the summer monsoons, and then experiences a winter drought. Furthermore, the natural savanna woodlands vegetation and grasslands have few nutrients for intensive grazing, the soils are poor, the region is a long distance from markets, and transport facilities are poorly developed. Thus, the land is used for little else except extensive beef cattle grazing on farms which sometimes exceed 15,000 square kilometres in size. The large size of the farms is needed because of the land's poor carrying capacity, which may mean one beast needs 20 to 30 hectares to survive. Attempts were made to establish irrigation agriculture around the Ord River in the 1960s, but saline soils, high costs of long distance transport to markets, and the costs of dam and irriga-

tion canal construction led to the virtual failure of the scheme in the early 1970s. It was intended to produce cotton, sugar cane and rice in the Ord River Scheme. Another land use, mining, is now of greater value than beef grazing. Important minerals include uranium (Rum Jungle, Ranger, Nabarlek), bauxite (Weipa, Mitchell Plateau), iron ore (Yampi Sound, Frances Creek), manganese (Groote Eylandt), copper, lead, silver, zinc (all at Mount Isa) and gold (Tennant Creek). The largest towns in the region are Darwin and Mount Isa, each with just over 35,000 people.

(S.B. & D.M. Codrington, *World of Contrasts: Case Studies in World Development for Secondary Geography*, William Brooks, Sydney, 1982, p. 193)

A cursory reading shows that the discussion is organised from a particular point of view in which different possibilities are weighed up and then placed in a particular way. A few examples will make the point: *The environmental conditions of this region mean that it is poorly suited to most forms of agriculture.* Here the major concern is 'suitability to agriculture', a concern which comes from a certain ideology: of ways of thinking about nature and the economy, of utility in relation to production, in short a certain kind of capitalist ideology. Other sentences in this brief extract are predictably enough quite similar: *the natural savanna woodlands vegetation and grasslands have few nutrients for intensive grazing . . . the region is a long distance from markets, and transport facilities are poorly developed; The large size of the farms is needed because of the land's poor carrying capacity.* These sentences, and the text as a whole, are constructed by a view which regards economic utility and exploitation as an unquestioned (natural) desire, and necessity.

By this I do not wish to make a point about western capitalism particularly, for a textbook from a socialist country for instance might talk in a quite similar fashion about a region of this kind. But it is easy to imagine other modes of writing this text. A somewhat different text could proceed from a standpoint with an emphasis on the physical conditions and then state what is possible within those conditions rather than here, where the possibilities of a certain form of economic use are prior values, and the land is classified in terms of them. A substantially different text would be written from the point of view of an environmentalist/ecological position with a quite different ideological system of values. It goes without saying that the Aboriginal inhabitants of this region (not classified as that kind of region by them, but by the colonists with their different culture) would find this text totally alien, written as it is from the standpoint of an incommensurate culture and ideology. A book just published, *Reading the Country*, provides Aboriginal accounts, 'readings', of what is now 'pastoral land' in the Kimberleys region of north-western Australia.

The text exemplifies a well-known effect of ideology, imposing a prior and systematically organised set of values on nature and on the objects of other cultures—as though they too were nature. The ideology here literally gives meaning to the land: *The environmental conditions of this region mean that*, a meaning which is totally at odds with the meaning given to the land in Aboriginal ideologies. This brief paragraph encapsulates, in its classificatory/ideological mode, the history and effects of one kind of imperialism.

See Benterrak, Muecke & Roe (1984).

69

Ideology affects—as does discourse—textual and syntactic form. Written from another ideological viewpoint, the text would have a different organisation. This would have syntactic consequences in two areas: for instance in terms of the thematic structuring of the text and of its constituent sentences, on the one hand, and in terms of structures of agency and causality on the other hand. An ideology which placed concern for the environment first, would lead to textual/syntactic forms which reflected these concerns. In other words, the assumed speaking position would entail certain assumed, taken-for-granted and therefore more or less implicit knowledge. That would affect decisions about what becomes thematic in a sentence, and what does not.

The first change of course would be in the classification: it would not be a *pastoral region*, as that classification derives from an economic discourse. Then, for instance, the first sentence could not remain as it is but might become something like: 'Most forms of agriculture are poorly suited to this region', with a differing emphasis, or 'Most forms of agriculture prove detrimental to this region'. With a more drastic ideological change, and a change of causality and agency structure the sentence might become 'The environmental conditions of this region prohibit most forms of agriculture', where the abstract category 'environmental conditions' has received agentive, causal powers. Clearly, consequential textual and syntactic alterations would arise for the rest of the text. In other words, ideology is not a matter of mere surface content as expressed in the kinds of words chosen but is everywhere entirely involved with the textual/syntactic aspects of a text. And as I implied above, in certain cultures and in their ideologies, this whole way of thinking about 'land' would not exist, that is, the subject could not even arise.

Metaphor and ideological struggle

In *Middlemarch* George Eliot has this to say about one of the characters in the novel, Mr Casaubon:

Poor Mr. Casaubon had imagined that his long studious bachelorhood had stored up for him a compound interest of enjoyment, and that large drafts on his affections would not fail to be honoured; for we all of us, grave or light, get our thoughts entangled in metaphors, and act fatally on the strength of them.

(G. Eliot, *Middlemarch*, Penguin Books, Harmondsworth, 1965)

Perhaps we, as modern Ms or Mr Casaubons, would not fall prey to this metaphor, knowing that affection and enjoyment are not like money and cannot be stored at interest as money can. For us, affection and enjoyment are integrated into different discourses, aligned with different ideologies. However, 'we all of us, grave or light, [still] get our thoughts entangled in metaphors'. For us, no less than for George Eliot, metaphor is a potent factor in ideological contention, a means to bring an area into one rather than another ideological domain.

Metaphor is also discussed by J.R. Martin in *Factual Writing: Exploring and Challenging Social Reality* (1989).

Metaphor works at all levels of language, from the largest textual/generic units to the smallest phonological features. Here I will briefly consider the metaphoric function and effect of prepositions.

George Eliot writes of getting *our thoughts entangled in metaphors, of acting fatally on the strength of them.* The prepositions *in* and *on* shift our thinking from the abstract to the spatial, turning the relation into one which is 'in' space: 'in', as opposed to 'by' for instance, which would make the relation into an instrumental rather than a spatial one. 'In' also makes 'metaphor' into a container, a net, where 'by' makes it into a tool. (Notice also my 'The prepositions *in* and *on* shift our thinking . . .' in the preceding sentence where 'shift' points to a spatial metaphor. In that sentence I employed another syntactic metaphor, suggesting that prepositions have the agentive power to 'shift our thinking', which at once turns 'thinking' into both an object-like entity, and one which is portrayed as being quite separate from the thinker.) These prepositions are metaphors by which we locate ourselves and everything else in space, time, or in instrumental relations with other objects.

These preposition/metaphors are basic to cultural classifications and hence to our thinking (note, by the way, my use of metaphor in 'basic'). Take 'up' and 'down', and the vast cluster of associations around each of these, and the two as a pair. There is a strong bias in favour of 'up'—perhaps because our parents were up, picked us up, and we resented being put down; we are exhorted to stand up and fight, or be counted; we would prefer to be looked up to, be feeling on the up-and-up, and we envy the upper crust, and hope that things will look up for us. Heaven is up, hell is down; the head and the heart are up, the genitals and excretary organs down. In our culture's dominant metaphor of sexual relations the male is up, on top of the female, as the sky is above the earth. Hence the metaphoric cluster of male/power/reason/good/light/ is opposed to the cluster of female/weak/irrational/wicked/dark. By a further metaphoric algebra light or fair skin is superior to dark skin, which supports the racist classifications that attend on the ideological valuations of colour.

I do not wish to labour the point here; no doubt it is clear enough from my brief discussion. Later in this chapter I will give a fairly extended analysis of the interrelation of ideology and syntactically-coded causality. In my view it is an instance of metaphor operating on the syntactic level. Metaphorical activity occurs at sites of difference, in struggles over power, whenever there is contention of an ideological kind, whenever an attempt is made to assimilate an event into one ideological system rather than another. A text that I have already discussed in Chapter I 'Squandering our inheritance' may illustrate this process:

Squandering our inheritance

We would have little respect for a young man who inherited great wealth but spent it so quickly that he died in poverty and left nothing to his heirs. But that is exactly the sort of thing the human race as a whole is doing today. We have inherited the earth and all it contains but we are using up its resources at a rate which, already alarming, is increasing rapidly. Unless drastic changes are made soon, our descendants will inherit a much poorer world.

(*Survival: Man and his World Book 4*, Macmillan, Melbourne, 1975, p. 199)

The title, itself a complex metaphor, sets the stage for the operation of the metaphor of 'husbanding of wealth' with its echoes of the profligate prodigal son. The ideological task and function are both equally clear; to bring the debate about the use of resources within one particular ideological position. As I mentioned in my analysis in Chapter I, a number of discourses operate in this text, and these are brought into a particular configuration by the moralist/conservationist ideology. The use of the metaphor is an attempt to locate the debate immediately, and to pre-empt any possibility of other alignments.

Metaphor is both ubiquitous in all linguistic activity, and essential to social life and to conceptual activity. In science, and in all attempts to construct knowledge, metaphor is a necessary strategy. It provides the means to step from the known to the unknown, from the well established to the new and hypothetical. I discussed this briefly in relation to the 'Man's part in soil erosion' text in Chapter 2. The following brief extract provides another illustration.

Insulator and charged body

In an insulator, the electrons do not move freely through the material. If a force is exerted on the electrons, only a slight change of their movements around the nuclei is induced.

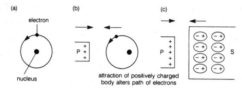

If a positively charged body, P, is brought near an insulator S, the electrons in S are attracted towards P but only slight distortion of the paths of some of the electrons results. An electron, which originally has a path as shown in (a) may have a path as shown in (b) when P is held nearby. Thus an electron in an atom of S, although still moving rapidly round its nucleus, will move a little more towards P.

The movement of the electrons in one direction means that the atom can be considered as a tiny rod with a negative charge at one end and a positive charge at the other. The net force on each atom of S is therefore towards P. Therefore there is a force of attraction between S and P, as in (c).

If free to do so, S and P will move towards each other and touch. There will be little transfer of charge from one body to the other because the electrons in S are not free to leave their atoms and transfer to P. Consequently the two objects remain attracted to each other.

(A. Boden et. al. *An Introduction to Science for High School Students*)

Here the first sentence in the third paragraph has that overt function: *The movement of the electrons in one direction means that the atom can be considered as a tiny rod. Atoms of course are not rods.* But the metaphor does bring a complex and abstract matter into the world of the everyday. Similarly with paths, which enables us to visualise a contested hypothesis in reassuringly homely terms.

The ideological construction of the social world

The ubiquitous action of metaphor is one force in the discursive and ideological process of 'naturalising' the social, of turning that which is problematic into the obvious. One large area of potential problems is the area of causality. 'Why do things happen?' and 'How do things happen?' are questions which fascinate children from the earliest age. The fact that these questions do not remain questions beyond childhood—except for a small group of specially designated people—is due to the classificatory, metaphoric and ultimately ideological effect of discourse. In language organised in discourse these questions are answered 'naturally' through the assignation of agency and causality to specific classes of objects. Here I wish to examine two instances of the operation of causality in texts. Both examples are from textbooks. The first is from E.E. Carpenter, *Home Management and House Care*; the second is a further extract from a book I have discussed previously, *Life B.C.* In each case the question is about the classification of processes, actions, and their effects. These are questions about a culture's assignation of the power to do certain things and to perform certain actions to classes of social agents and to abstract entities (who may, by metaphoric transfer, come to seem to be social agents). Children, in learning language through their experience of texts, come to learn the classifications, the assignment of power, and see them as 'natural'.

Home management and house care

    . . . powder, or by a combination of these methods. In some instances electrolytic action will remove tarnish, e.g. silver dip cleaners.

    Light soil is easy to remove while it is fresh. When allowed to accumulate, it hardens and harsher treatments are needed to remove it,
5   which may harm the surface underneath. Regular cleaning is quick and easy and involves only simple inexpensive cleaning supplies. The task can be lightened further if simple sturdy materials are chosen for the various household surfaces.

Household cleansers

10 Abrasives
These are mechanical cleaners which abrade or grind the surface, assisting in removal of soil, tarnish, stains etc. Unless chosen and used carefully, they may damage the surface.

Examples
15 Fine abrasives—volcanic ash, feldspar.
Medium abrasives—whiting, powdered pumice or rottenstone.
Coarse abrasives—sand, quartz.

Absorbents
Some fine powders can absorb liquids or grease and when they are
20 removed, by brushing or vacuuming, the soil goes too.

Examples
Cornflour, talcum powder, french chalk, bran, fuller's earth.

Acids
These have the power to dissolve tarnish and other deposits and may
25 also act as bleaches. They are often used in conjunction with an abrasive substance such as salt or scouring powder.

Examples

Lemon juice, vinegar, cream of tartar, oxalic acid.

Hydrochloric acid (spirits of salts) is a very strong acid used for drastic
30   cleaning, e.g. lavatory bowls, brick fireplaces.

Alkalis

These react with grease and make it into an emulsion which dissolves in
water, carrying soil with it. They also soften hard water by changing
its mineral salts to soluble forms, thus preventing scums forming with soap.

35   ### Examples

Ammonia, a solution of ammonia gas in water (household ammonia). With
a little soap added, this is sold as cloudy ammonia. If the latter is
used, rinse well to avoid leaving a film. Used for cleaning carpets,
upholstery, brushes. Avoid on aluminium, sisal, and test on coloured
40   fabrics first.

Baking soda (sodium bicarbonate), a mild alkaline powder used as a fine
abrasive for enamel, porcelain, plastic.

Borax (sodium tetraborate), mild alkali, water softener and fine abrasive.
Uses as for baking soda.

45   Caustic soda (sodium hydroxide), a very strong alkali. Will corrode
aluminium, enamel and porcelain glazes.

Trisodium phosphate, a moderately strong alkali, effective as a water
softener and for removing grease. It is the active ingredient in some paint
removers. Avoid excess as this may harm some surfaces.

50   Washing soda (sodium carbonate), cheap and effective as a grease
solvent and water softener, but can harm wood, metal, paint etc. if not
used in correct proportions, or rinsed away completely.

Bleaches

These are often used to lighten discoloured surfaces or to remove stains.
55   Apply only as directed, as misuse can be harmful.

Examples

Chlorine bleaches, formerly only available as liquids, but now also in
powder form. Also called household bleaches, they contain sodium
hypochlorite and are strong bleaches used to whiten wood, baths and
60   basins, white cottons and linens. Not suitable for silk, wool, synthetics,
drip-dry or crease-resist finishes. Chlorine bleaches also act as disin-
fectants.

Hydrogen peroxide is a mild bleach useful for whitening baths and
removing stains from all fabrics. It must be fresh, as it loses its effective-
65   ness with time.

Sodium perborate, a mild powder bleach, suitable for all fabrics. It works
slowly at cool temperatures and requires longer application.

Grease solvents

This class of cleanser acts by dissolving grease and evaporating,
70   carrying the soil with it. Use with caution, as they are often flam-
mable, or poisonous, or both.

(Emily E. Carpenter, *Home Management and House Care*, Whitcoulls
Publishers, New Zealand, 1977, pp. 108–9)

One of the major concerns of the text is classification, in the sense discussed in Chapter 3; that is, it attempts to define and describe one aspect of the world of 'the home' and of 'house care'. In this, the text provides a set of terms and of definitions: *Borax (sodium tetraborate), mild alkali, water softener and fine abrasive. Uses as for baking soda.* This provides a multiple classification for the term (and the substance) 'Borax', tying it into classificatory categories judged as relevant: into the scientific through the chemical name and classification as a mild alkali; into the domestic through the descriptions of its functions as water softener and abrasive; and tying it too, cohesively, into knowledge which is assumed as established by the instruction *Uses as for baking soda.* In establishing these classifications, the text also indirectly establishes (or reinforces) the more important classifications of the types of activities which are included in 'housecare'. To take one example, the category of *Bleaches.* The term itself suggests one kind of activity; the description of the term *Hydrogen peroxide* provides further instructions/classification: *is a mild <u>bleach</u> useful for <u>whitening baths</u> and <u>removing stains from all fabrics.</u>*

So while the text is ostensibly about describing the terms of one classificatory system, more significantly it is about the classification of kinds of actions which have relevance in this domain. The question then arises about who is assigned causal powers and agency in this domain of relevance? The answer is somewhat complex. Take for instance line 24 *These have the power to dissolve tarnish and other deposits.* Here there is a direct description of acids as having *power*; and the syntax supports this in that acids is the subject agent of the verb *dissolve* and directly affects *tarnish.* (I will call clauses such as this, which are transitive in syntax and in meaning, 'transactive'). The second, conjoined, clause in this sentence *and may also act as bleaches* is also transactive, though here the agentive power of *acids* is modified by the modal *may.* The next sentence, line 25, *They are often used in conjunction with an abrasive substance such as,* is a clause which is also transactive, in the passive voice; the unstated agent here however is not acids, but the unspecified and unknown 'user' of the acids. Here power and agency therefore rest with the 'user'.

The reading position constructed in this text is one in which the reader is encouraged to identify with the absent, unstated agent, as in the sentence just discussed or in numerous others here, for instance lines 3–8 *Light soil is easy [for you] to remove . . . When allowed [by you] . . . harsher treatments [by you] . . . [for you] to remove it . . . Regular cleaning [by you] is quick [for you] and easy [for you] and involves [you] . . . The task can be lightened [by you] . . . are chosen [by you].* The situation is therefore one where agency and causal power are distributed between the 'you' constructed in the reading position (and here it is important whether the readers of this text are likely to be predominantly male or female) and the *Household cleansers.* The sentence (from line 3 on) I have just analysed is in that respect entirely typical. To take one other example (lines 11–13) *These are mechanical cleaners which abrade or grind the surface, assisting in removal of soil, tarnish, stains etc. Unless chosen and used carefully, they may damage the surface.* The cleaners are agentive in abrading, grinding or damaging the surface. 'You' is agentive in the passive *If the latter is used [by you]*, in the transactive *[you] rinse [it] well, [you] avoid leaving a film, [you] avoid on aluminium*.

The system which seems to be operating here is as follows: agency may be assigned **either** to the human 'you' (*Light soil is easy to remove*) **or** to the cleansing agent (*[Acids] have the power to dissolve tarnish*). In other words either kind of agent can act independently. Where a task is to be performed which does not involve the use of a cleanser, or which is described in a way that avoids mention of a cleanser, 'you' is given agency. Where the task involves cleanser without a human cleaner being involved, the cleanser is given agency. Where both are mentioned, that is, where the task is described/classified in such a way as to involve both, the human agent is not mentioned, by the use of an agentless passive—line 41 *a mild alkaline powder used as a*; or by the use of a nominalisation—line 44 *Uses as for*, line 12 *in removal of soil*, line 29 *drastic cleaning*, line 55 *as misuse can be harmful*; or by the use of non-finite forms of the verb—line 38 *rinse well*, line 39 *Avoid on . . . and test on*, line 54 *to remove stains*. In other words, where both kinds of agent are involved, the cleanser agent is given prominence textually, and the human agent is backgrounded textually. Syntactically, human agency generally 'precedes' and dominates the agency of the physical agents; lines 12–13 *Unless chosen and used carefully, they may damage the surface*. Here the fully restored form is 'Unless <u>you</u> choose and use them carefully, they . . .'. However, to recover this form involves a very deliberate act of reading.

Here I want to insist on the point that this is not a necessary assignment of agency; other systems are readily imaginable: for instance one where human agency is much more or even totally prominent or dominant, or perhaps one in which human agency is totally absent (as in certain kinds of advertisements). The decisions to have one system rather than another are ideological ones, related entirely to the kinds of social and economic structures of a given society. For instance in western technological societies, women's roles are still largely constructed within sexist discourse. Among very many other things this suggests that domestic labour is 'women's work'. At the same time it is suggested by technological and by certain economic discourses that domestic labour is really no longer labour because of the thorough permeation of technological aids in domestic labour, and that therefore women are free and able to join the workforce. Hence the reality of women's domestic labour has to be acknowledged on the one hand—lest men lose some of their power, and on the other hand it has to be insisted—in this case by a pedagogical ideologue—that women's work is not in any serious sense labour, because technology has intervened in the structure of domestic life and has taken away the need for women's domestic labour.

These social, economic and ideological necessities coincide neatly with the needs of the capitalist economy for ever-increasing production and consequently, consumption. This part of the ideological process is filled by the advertising industry, whose function it is to produce consumers. Some of the strategies of the advertising industry are broadly similar to those of this text, though somewhat differently motivated.

76

In many areas, the commodities which it describes have agentive powers ascribed to them, so that they promise the benefits of technology to the consumer. At the same time, the consumer/user must feel 'in control', must not feel threatened by the powers of the commodity. Nor does the advertising industry wish to disrupt sexist discourse, as that in its turn produces the subjects (with specific subject positions) which advertising can address, and around which its strategies for producing consumers are based. The picture is more complex than I can here attempt to deal with; for instance feminist discourse is both a challenge to advertising by undermining the discourses which have supported it, and at the same time holds out the promise of delivering a new audience, and a new class of consumers.

The point I wish to make here is that the school textbook reflects the ideological categories of the economic and social system into which the child readers are being socialised so closely, and indeed mirrors the texts and strategies of the world of advertising. For instance, a few, randomly chosen examples, yield the following:

Helps remove stains in the wash
With BIO JOY most stains come out in the wash
Just put it in with your normal detergent
And for more difficult stains there's a simple chart on the back of the pack
Used either as a detergent booster in the wash or as a laundry soaker, BIO
JOY does the work for you

(*New Idea*, 6.9.1984, p. 124)

or, from the label on a bottle of household cleaner:

AJAX SPRAY N' WIPE,
All purpose solvent cleaner
Cleans without rinsing

In other words, the school text constructs the subject positions and reading positions, constructs the ideal readers and the audience/ consumers for the world of advertising. Clearly this facilitates the work of advertising and the creation of consumers enormously; in a real sense this text of this curriculum area delivers audiences to the world of advertising ready made.

Whereas the ideological arrangement of discourses in this text operates in the main with clearly transactive categories, assigning agency now to one class of agents and now to another, other texts show other ideological orderings. Here I will briefly discuss an extract from *Life B.C.*

Life B.C.

Empire

Rome had grown and prospered under the Republic. But around the middle of the first century B.C. the Republic began to break down. Some individuals had become too powerful.
5   Two Roman generals, Julius Caesar and Pompey, even went to war against each other. Caesar won, but some Senators thought he was becoming too powerful and murdered him.

Fighting continued between Romans until Octavian gained control
of the army. In 27 B.C. he changed his name to Augustus and made
10 himself Emperor. Augustus told the people that he was ending the times
of trouble by going back to the old ways. He brought back many of the
old ways in religion. In politics he introduced many new ways.

He ruled Rome as if he were king. The Senate and Assemblies
continued but all they did was advise the king. Augustus held power by
15 taking over all the most important positions in government himself. He
then hired men to put into action the laws he made. He also ruled the
many lands which the Roman army had conquered.

As the head of an Empire, Rome became enormously rich. Wealth
brought problems. Too many poor people moved into Rome. Unem-
20 ployment was severe. Emperors like Nero and Caligula were cruel.
Rome had become an impressive looking city with magnificent buildings
and engineering achievements. But the people had no say in their own
government.

The empire continued until the time that Rome was destroyed by
25 barbarians in A.D. 455.

(G. Garden, *Life B.C.*, Heinemann Educational Australia, 1980, p. 130)

I mentioned above that the assignment of agency is conventional
to some extent, or, somewhat more precisely, is not determined by an
unproblematic relationship with 'reality'. In a history text one would
expect to find transactive clauses to be predominant, as they give the
clearest syntactic indication of causality, of who did what to whom. This
text is remarkably devoid of causative constructions. Most clauses are
non-transactive, that is, are clauses which indicate or describe an action
without indicating either cause or effect. So for instance in
line 2 *Rome had grown and prospered under the Republic, growing* and
prospering are shown as taking place, happening, but without any
indicated cause. Similarly with (line 3) *the Republic began to break down.*
This is presented as a self-caused, spontaneous event. Obviously there
were complex causes at work; but this text presents, through the syntax,
a picture of a world where 'things just happen'. Other examples abound:
line 4 *Some individuals had become too powerful*; line 8 *Fighting
continued between Romans*, lines 13—14 *The Senate and Assemblies
continued*; line 18 *Rome became enormously rich*, etc. There are some
transactives, predominantly associated with Augustus as agent; or, line
18, *Wealth brought problems* which, while it is a transactive, uses
nominalisations as agent and affected in such a way that human causality
is not recoverable.

It may be felt that I am missing the point here, namely that this
is simplifed history, written for simple, unsophisticated readers, whose
interest would not be held by more complex structures of causality.
I would not agree with such a comment anyway, as it severely misjudges
children's abilities to handle complexities. More significant however is
the point that if this is a student's first introduction to history, she or
he will take away a very peculiar perception of what that discipline is
about—a discipline founded on causal accounts whose texts proceed
in largely acausal terms. The syntactic metaphor created here is directly
at odds with the ostensible aims of the discipline.

Ideology and the clash of discourses

In the cases which I have discussed so far, ideology has functioned to bring different discourses into particular configurations which are by and large mutually supportive. The ideological task may be to bring incommensurable discourses into the one text and there to attempt some resolution of the difference, in whichever direction. My next example is an instance of one such case. It is a letter/memorandum written by the Director-General of Education in an Australian State to Principals of departmental schools, in 1970. The title of the letter indicates the clash at issue.

To Principals of all Departmental Schools
Freedom and Authority in the Schools
I have been asked to define more clearly what is meant by the freedom you and your staff have been exhorted to use in the schools. I shall be grateful if you will make the contents of this memorandum known to your staff.
5 Let me say at the outset that you as Head of your school, by delegated authority from the Minister and the Director-General, are in undisputed control of your school.
Within the broad framework of the Education Act, the general curriculum advised by the curriculum boards and approved by me as
10 Director-General of Education, and the general policy set by the Director of your Division and communicated to you by circular, you have the widest liberty to vary courses, to alter the timetable, to decide the organisation of the school and government within the school, to experiment with teaching methods, assessment of student achievement and in extra-
15 curricular activities.
Grouping, setting, streaming, development of tracks, block time-tabling and ungrading are all acceptable schemes of organisation. Cooperative teaching, team teaching, tutorials and independent study are all acceptable methods for teaching and learning.
20 In any experiment or variations the general well-being and education of the students must be the prime concern. Consequently any major change should be with the full knowledge of parents.
In exercising your authority and freedom to run your school as you think fit, of necessity you must have the backing of your staff. Without
25 their support and participation and their adequate preparation, any departures from tradition will have little chance of success.
Just as you have professional freedom and delegated authority, so too the same privileges should be extended to your staff, who in turn must accept your ultimate authority in the school and the stake that
30 parents and students have in what goes on in the schools.
Staff members will more readily follow a course of action if they have been taken into confidence and have shared in formulating the policy. They will be less effective and less enthusiastic if they feel that communication is all one way and their voices are not heard.
35 With any innovation it is expected that the motive is to meet more effectively the needs of students. A sound reason for rejecting, say, a

trial of 'setting' English or Mathematics or indeed of classes in any given subject, might be that there were insufficient teachers of the appropriate kind available at the one time to organise it. An unsound reason would
40 be that 'setting' is perhaps more difficult to arrange administratively.

No experiment must commit the Education Department to supply more staff, more accommodation, more equipment or more funds without prior consultation. Nor must parents be put to expense without their concurrence.

45 The question of government in a school is of prime importance, and should therefore make provision, especially in secondary schools, for student opinion to make itself known. Ways of bringing this about will differ with the size and nature of each school, and the relative age and maturity of the student concerned. Methods are best left for the schools
50 to work out.

Finally, the sooner the old concept of the fixed timetable and strictly regulated movement as the blueprint of the school day disappears, the better.

The timetable should reflect a great variety of individual approaches.
55 The timetable should be the servant of the curriculum, and both be servants to the student.

A.W. Jones
Director-General of Education

I discussed an extract from this text in Chapter 3, and the forms to which I drew attention there characterise the rest of the text. The many agentless passives here serve to avoid specifying certain individuals or groups, whose prohibitions constitute a part of the problematic of the text. These absent agents speak with and as the voice of authority; lines 1–2 *the freedom you and your staff have been <u>exhorted</u> to use*; lines 5–7 *you . . . are in undisputed control*; i.e. a control not disputed and freedom exhorted by the 'authorities'. They are in contention with a largely absent discourse of freedom, which appears in this text by negation, modification, modulation largely, and of course as a major motivation of the text.

So for instance the text shows a consistent distinction in modalities between an unambiguously authoritative 'must' and a vaguely concessive 'should': lines 20–22 *In any experiment . . . education . . . <u>must</u> be the prime concern. Consequently any major change <u>should</u> be with the knowledge of parents,* or lines 27–29 *so too the same privileges should be <u>extended</u> to your staff, who in turn <u>must</u> accept your ultimate authority,* and other examples.

This clash of discourses is carried in the causality structures. I have already mentioned the force of the agentless passives. Definitional clausal forms, 'X is Y', express power by the establishment of classifications as states of being. Lines 5–7 *you . . . <u>are</u> in undisputed control*; lines 16–17 *Grouping, setting, . . . <u>are</u> all acceptable*; lines 20–21 *education . . . must <u>be</u> the prime concern*; lines 33–34 *They will <u>be</u> less effective . . . communication <u>is</u> all one way*; line 35 *the motive <u>is</u> to meet*; line 46 *The question . . . <u>is</u> of prime importance.* These forms issue from an unquestionable authority, as unchallengeable descriptions which act as directives. This is the same authority as that which is the source of the *must's* discussed above.

80

But as in the housecare example, agentiveness, and with it authority, is not uniformly assigned to one participant. The reader addressed in the text has agentive powers. Lines 11—13 *you have the widest liberty to vary courses, to alter the timetable, to decide the organisation of the school*; here the subject of the non-finite transactive clauses is in each case 'you'; and 'you' is also the implied subject of the nominalisation *organisation of the school*—i.e. 'you organise the school'. Similarly with, for instance, line 16 *Grouping, setting, streaming* which also have 'you' as the implied subject 'you group, stream, set . . .'. The strategy is pervasive in this text. One last and yet again differing example: lines 23—24 *In exercising your authority and freedom to run your school as you think fit.* Here *authority* and *freedom* are classified as instrumental entities, quite discrete and separate from the individual, seen as possessions of the individual in the same way as the more concrete *your school* is also. All three can therefore be subject to the agentive force of the possessor, who can 'exercise her/his authority' much as she or he might exercise their dog, and 'run their school' much as they might run their car.

The discourse of authority is therefore very clearly marked in the syntax of causality. The discourse of freedom appears somewhat less clearly in the syntax. Lines 45—47 are characteristic of the vagueness with which it is handled here: *The question of government in a school is of prime importance, and should therefore make provision, especially in secondary schools, for student opinion to make itself known.* The syntax is exceedingly vague here; for instance, what is the subject of *make provision*? The only possibility is *The question of government*; but that does not make a syntactically or semantically satisfactory subject. Clearly the writer had some ideologically troubling problems here—unless we assume that the Director-General's knowledge of syntax is not adequate to the task of writing the memo, which is an implausible hypothesis. The vagueness concerns causality: who precisely should make this provision, and how should it be made? The non-transactive, acausal syntax of *for student opinion to make itself known*, suggesting some spontaneous, unspecific mode of action, is a further demonstration of the point. In this context the qualifying phrase *especially in secondary schools* acts as a further weakening: it seems to be the surface indicator of a debate about whether this should be the case in all levels of schooling, a debate which was resolved against primary school children and with qualified support of 'opinion making itself known' in secondary schools. Nor is *Ways of bringing this about* clear on causality, either on the level of syntax or in any other way. The syntax of the last sentence embodies this vagueness; the agentless passive *Methods are best left* leaves the question precisely of who the agent is who leaves this decision *for the schools to work out.* That last phrase, while its causality is syntactically precise ('schools work out methods') leaves the problem of vague causality by transposing it to the subject noun *schools*. It is entirely unclear what consultative processes, lines of communication, structures of authority, not to mention 'exercises of freedom' can and will be involved in this. The writer's own exasperation and bewilderment seems to be well expressed in the (yet again acausal) *the sooner the old concept . . . disappears, the better.*

In as far as the discourse of freedom appears in the text syntactically, it therefore appears as an entirely vague notion; that is, the syntax gives no indication at all of what specific processes would be or are entailed in actions within this freedom. In as far as there are indications in the syntax they are acausal: 'things just happen'. The syntax suggests anarchy, not freedom. Syntactically therefore the discourse of freedom appears by its negation, in the various forms that I have mentioned. Just some brief examples will illustrate how 'freedom' appears at the level of teachers, parents and children. Lines 27–29 may serve as a summary: *Just as you have professional freedom and delegated authority, so too the same privileges should be extended to your staff, who in turn must accept your ultimate authority. The contrast of modalities in privileges should be extended [by you] to your staff and [they] in turn must accept your ultimate authority* indicates that the attempted parallel and analogy 'just as . . . so too . . .' has no validity. Staff can offer *their support and participation* (line 25), and are permitted to have *adequate preparation [by you?]*; they may *more readily follow* (line 31); and may (line 32) *have shared in formulating the policy*. They may also be *enthusiastic* and will, it is hoped, be *effective* (line 33). All of these are non-transactive processes and clauses; that is, the subjects of these processes are **not** causal agents, do not (directly) control the processes or affect other entities.

There is a clear hierarchy of power and authority coded in the syntax. The unnamed authority of the agentless passives, and the named authority of the Education Act, of the Minister, of the curriculum boards, and of the Director-General exercise and delegate authority; this is 'exercised' by the principals in 'their' schools, within limits described. Both kinds of agent have power and authority and can be causally active and effective. 'Below' this level the syntax suggests that others may share, follow, be enthusiastic, and participate, but not act in a causally effective manner.

Notions of 'freedom' are articulated and elaborated at a more overt level, in words, phrases, 'ways of saying'. So there is mention of *co-operative teaching, team teaching, . . . independent study* (line 18); the *prime concern* is *the general well-being . . . of the students* (lines 20–21); talk of *support and participation*, of taking staff members into confidence, of two way communication, and so on. In other words, the catch phrases of more liberal educational thinking and practice are there; but they remain superficial flourishes.

The clash of the two discourses gives rise to the text. It is an ideology of control which places the two in relation to each other in this text: the discourse of authority is coded in the syntax, that is, at the deepest, most fundamental linguistic level; the discourse of freedom is 'there' by negations, is syntactically coded as anarchic, and coded also on the surface in words and phrases which are recognisable indices of certain discourses on liberal education.

Ideology and the plausibility of common sense

In Chapter 1, I posed the question: How and why do texts get produced? My initial answers focused on discourses and on discursively-constructed difference, and on the function and effect of genre. Discourse and genre account for what is there in the text, but between them do not and cannot fully account for **how** what is there is there. In other words, how is it decided how differing discourses occurring in one text are to be aligned, articulated, ordered in a particular text? Ideology provides particular configurations and co-articulations of discourses; indicates preferred matchings of certain discourses with certain genres and strives towards the achievement of plausible, commonsense texts. While discourse and genre provide the systematically-organised linguistic categories which make up a text, ideology determines the configuration of discourses that are present together and their articulation in specific genres. Ideology is therefore intricately connected into the construction of texts. For instance, in the last example discussed in the preceding section of this chapter two discourses are present together, and are given form in a particular genre, that of a circular/memorandum. These provide the linguistic categories and forms which appear in the text. However, it is ideology which indicates how the two discourses are to be valued, or ranged in relation to each other, how their contention is to be resolved, to what extent and how either is to appear in the text. While discourses arise out of and encode the meanings of particular institutions, ideologies determine the arrangement of discourses in text (and of texts other than linguistic as well as linguistic texts) in response to the demands of larger social structures. In the last example the writer, and the institution he served, clearly felt that the two discourses needed to be put into a certain relation with each other. In the late 1960s new discourses on education were challenging the established educational discourse. The text is a result of that challenge, in an attempt (not unlike the 'Miss Mouse'/'Ms Winner' texts from *Cleo*) to bring the challenge within the established discourse, and thereby to contain it.

Ideology determines the configuration of discourses present and their articulation in specific genres.

In such attempts ideology is always conservative. The sense that it makes of the social world is the sense derived from established social and material practices. The meanings of any ideological system are therefore always the meanings of the past. Whenever there is change (other than revolutionary change) ideology provides the categories which shape any thinking about the new practices. While the practices may be new—arising through technological changes or by 'importation'—the categories used to think about the practices and to classify them are the established, comfortable categories of a well-understood past, about which there **is** a common sense. Innumerable occasions of the regulation of contending or complementary discourses in texts create what becomes the common sense *vis-à-vis* given areas for any one cultural, social group. That is, in the texts of a social group the interrelation of discourses tend to be resolved in broadly similar ways, so that that which habitually happens in texts comes to be the common meaning, the common sense.

At the same time, as material and social practices alter, that ideologically-constructed common sense is always out of phase with these practices. There is thus a constant tension between social reality and social practices and the way in which they are and can be written or talked about in languge. In texts these differences can be made overt, can be made the subject of new classification. In this way material practices continue to affect and shape cultural ideological categories, those of language included. Here, in this difference and in this constant dialogue lies the motor of social change, and therefore of linguistic change.

This view accounts for a number of seeming paradoxes: the stability of the linguistic system and its constant change; the autonomy of language, of discourse and of ideology, and their complete 'at oneness' with the whole social system. Perhaps most significantly it accounts for the active and shaping role of individual speakers and writers, hearers and readers in relation to the momentum of a socially-determined complex of structures.

Chapter 5

Social processes and linguistic change: time and history in language

The discursive construction of linguistic history: Saussure and his readers

Much of my argument so far has been constructed around the apparent paradox of the social determination of linguistic processes on the one hand and the significance of individual linguistic action on the other. The paradox remains as long as we think of the social (and with it the linguistic system) outside time, 'out of time'. It then has the appearance of a static, fixed system. Such 'snapshot views' underlie the most influential theory in this area in this century, that of Ferdinand de Saussure. He had spent his early years as a scholar working within the last significant period of the study of the histories of (mainly) European languages. His own early work represented an important consolidation of the monumental achievements of nearly a century of intensive research in Europe. Historical linguistics of the nineteenth century was concerned to show the relationship between European languages by tracing each to an assumed common ancestry, and to demonstrate the regularities governing language changes. In that process it demonstrated the 'family' connections between languages as distant as modern Hindi, long-extinct Middle-Eastern languages such as Hittite, and European languages such as Russian, Italian, German, and English, through their links with languages such as ancient Sanskrit and Greek for instance. What this work revealed and inevitably focused on was language as a system constantly in a process of change.

Against this picture of a diachronous system, seen in and through time, subject to constant change, Saussure posited the notion of the synchronous language system with time held still momentarily, a system of regularity and internal consistency, fixed and not subject to change. That was the picture put forward by Saussure in a series of lectures given at the University of Geneva. These were later edited from their lecture notes by two of Saussure's students, Charles Bally and Albert Sechehaye, and published by them after Saussure's death as the enor-

David Butt discusses the work of Saussure in *Talking and Thinking: the Patterns of Behaviour* (1989).

85

mously influential *Course in General Linguistics*. It needs to be said at once that this book contains the contradictions that I have outlined, the unresolved opposition of diachrony and synchrony, and with it the unresolved opposition of language as a socially and historically determined phenomenon and language as an autonomous system. In my view it is quite unclear how Saussure might have resolved these tensions had he written the book himself—the book is after all a compilation from lecture notes by two students who were making **their** sense, their reading of these lectures. In the book there is a constant tension between these contradictory tendencies, sufficient to suggest that these matters were not settled for Saussure.

What **is** clear however is how the book has been read consistently since then. One reading, that of the synchronous autonomous system, outside time and outside of its social historical context, has been predominant. In that reading the individual language user meets the system as a monolithic, immutable given, which she or he may use but cannot alter. By and large this is the view of the individual's relation which has continued to hold sway, explicitly or implicitly.

My reason for giving this little history is a two-fold one. Firstly, I think that it provides a rather neat example of my discussion in the preceding chapters of the effects of discourses and ideologies on writing **and** on reading. Saussure's text is constructed precisely out of and in the difference between contradictory discourses: the romantic nineteenth-century discourses of freedom, change and of the social (in this case language) as a species of the natural, and the discourses (embodied in this case in the writings, for instance, of Durkheim) of the rule-governed system, of the social as subject to its own laws, and of the individual as subject to the social. The fact that one reading proved predominant is explained in my account by the predominance of the latter set of discourses at the time when Saussure's lectures appeared as a written, objectified text. What seems to have been very much a live dialogue for Saussure himself became for his readers a settled unidimensional text. Secondly, I believe that it is both important and helpful to see the historical, ideological and discursive constructedness of views which have taken on the mantle of the obvious. Awareness of this kind allows us to find a different, our own, reading position, and with that some useful space for independent analysis and thinking.

In this case it is the role of the individual *vis-à-vis* social and linguistic processes that I wish to focus on, and to locate in a different discourse.

Speakers as agents of linguistic change

There are no doubt very many ways in which linguistic change can be thought about. In this chapter, I will focus on just two: a change to the ideological, discursive and generic position of individual speakers, in other words a change to the 'linguistic make-up' of individuals; and a change to the linguistic system through changes in discourses, genres and ideologies brought about by 'speaking agents'.

Every text involves development, progression, and change. It is one of the demands of texts that there is change. This can appear in quite trivial ways; for instance, as I read back over my manuscript I eliminate repetitions. Where I find that I have written the same word twice within reasonably close proximity I change one to a near synonym. So for instance I have quite recently changed a repeated use of *significant* to *important*. The conventional explanation for that is that repetitions 'jar'; though I myself do not find that repetition jarring. I suspect that the real reason is that repetition signals absence of development and progression, and thus contravenes a fundamental convention of texts.

Progression is a formal characteristic of most genres. Take this little narrative written, or typed rather, by a seven-year-old boy.

Seven-year-old boy's narrative

    Once upon a time there lived two poeple axnd their son.
    they were verxy̶x̶x̶x̶x̶ poor.
    In their ganden they groo cavig and bens..
    One day they looked in their muny bocxks and there wxxxas
5   onlex
    One xpene in it.
    What shal we do?
    xWe will have to sell the table.
    Tomorrow we will sell in the market.
10 The x̶x̶x̶x̶x̶ next day the boy went to the market.
    He sold the table but there was not anuf muny.
    He was just x̶x̶ xx about to go home wxhen he notist that
    the xxxstall x̶x̶x̶x̶ next-door was selling some thing
    difrnt.
15 He went to the stall and xxx said what are x̶x̶x̶x̶x̶x̶x̶ you
    selling.
    We are selling pots pans and friing-pans.
    How much is that pot it is 4 penes Iwill bx̶y it.
    xxx It was a hot sony day so he put his coat in it.
20 When he got home he looked in the pot and there was two coat's.
    Daddy look mummy look then they tuck one coat out.
    And anuth coat aperd then they put their shous in and
       there was twis-as many as befro.
    THey solld shoescoat's and hats.
25 they lived happly ever rft..

The progression is obvious, and generically determined: from description of initial state, to complication/crisis, to resolution and final inversion of the initial situation: *One day they looked in their muny bocks and there was onle one pene in it*, to: *They solld shoescoat's and hats. they lived happly every rft . . . .* The conventionality might obscure the real significance of this text, namely that there is thoroughgoing progression throughout the text, which proceeds with an algebraic precision. The constant and insistent experience of such texts suggests to the child that in texts 'something always happens', that things at the end are not what they were at the beginning. This experience sets up a pattern of expectation for all texts. Texts that do not meet this expectation are considered inconclusive, repetitive, texts which 'don't get anywhere'. These are negative judgments in Anglo-Australian culture; though there is no reason why other cultures might not attach different valuations to such texts.

The two important points are: firstly, the habitually-established expectation of 'progression', that progression of time also implies progression of some other kind. That is a deeply-coded notion in western thought, and narrative is just one, though a most important instance of it. Secondly, the writer is the agent of the progression. So although the genre demands progression, the writer implements the genre, and thereby causes there to be progression in the text. The individual therefore is the one who causes progression in the text. When this becomes generalised to all texts the importance of the point is obvious: individuals are causally involved in progression and change, and consequently where that progression or change affects the formal constitution of discourse or genre, it is still the individual who is agentive in this process.

Education is quintessentially about the progression and change of individuals in relation to dominant systems of classification. That progression is most visible in interactively-constructed texts. Here is an example from a childcare centre. The three participants are the teacher, Sarah (who is four years and six months old) and Aaron (who is four years and five months old). After an initial discussion about bedwetting between Aaron, Sarah and the teacher, the talk focuses on the pictures on a poster the teacher has been pinning up.

Talk

Teacher: Look at this (pointing to picture of mother and young rhino)
Sarah: His mother s a lot of toothes.
Teacher: How many teeth? How many have they got?
5   Sarah: one two three, four
Teacher: What are they up the top?
Sarah: One two three four five
Teacher: Five at the top and four at the bottom
Aaron: No they're pimples
10 Teacher: Do you think they're pimples?
Aaron: Yeah
Teacher: But they're where his teeth should be . . . do you think they're just a different colour?
Aaron: Well . . . that . . . those are pimples cos those are
15   pink
Teacher: Um . . . could be too . . . and what do you call those things there?
Sarah: Whiskers
Teacher: You do too and what's that Sarah?
20 Sarah: A ear
Teacher: It's a funny looking ear isn't it?
Aaron: Yes . . . a little ear
Sarah: Thats got two . . . one, two . . . two ears
Teacher: Do you think they'd be friendly? . . . these
25   rhinoceroses?

88

```
        Aaron & Sarah:  No
        Teacher: Why not?
        Aaron:    Cos they'll eat people
        Teacher: How do you know? What makes them look unfriendly?
30      Aaron:    Their teeth . . . they can eat people
        Teacher: They are big. What about this animal?
        Sarah:    That hasn't got any teeth
        Teacher: Hasn't he?
        Sarah:    No
35      Teacher: Do you think he'd be friendly?
        Sarah & Aaron:  Yes
        Teacher: Look what he has got
        Sarah:    He's got little claws
        Teacher: Claws
40      Sarah:    See . . . but that . . . but he's still our friendly . . .
        Teacher: He's still friendly even if he's got claws?
        Sarah:    Look . . . they're not flendry
        Aaron:    Yes they are
        Teacher: Do you think lions are friendly Aaron?
45      Aaron:    Yeah . . . because . . . if they . . . if people hurt them they
                  hurt them back
        Teacher: And it's quite safe you think if you don't hurt them?
        Aaron:    Yes
        Teacher: I don't know
```

This extract shows a series of textual episodes constructed around the introduction of a (classificatory) term and a brief exchange about its integration into one classificatory system or another. For instance, in lines 3–16 Sarah introduces *toothes*. The teacher implicitly accepts this classification (of a part of the picture) by the question of how many teeth there are. Aaron challenges the classification, line 9, *No they're pimples*. The interaction now focuses on two differing classificatory principles, the teacher's authoritative (note the *should*) *they're where his teeth should be* and Aaron's *cos those are pink*. The teacher does not accept Aaron's classification, leaving the matter unresolved: *Um . . . could be too . . .* To take another example, lines 31–49. Here the question is whether lions are to be classified as friendly or not, and on what grounds. The teacher's principle seems to be that 'claws' indicates the category 'unfriendly'; Sarah seems to equate absence of teeth with friendliness; and Aaron's principle seems to involve the question whether the animal initiates the unfriendliness or merely acts in retaliation. The teacher again leaves the question of which classification system 'lion' is to be assigned to up in the air; though as she indicates her agreement quite clearly in other cases (lines 19,21) the children are no doubt aware of the absence of the teacher's agreement.

Clearly there is progression in these examples: it is not overtly carried to one conclusion, though there will be other occasions when the status of these terms will be raised again. At issue here are the systems of linguistic and cultural valuations. The teacher acts as an agent of cultural reproduction, though the children too are active in this process. In this text the two children attempt to sustain their classification; the teacher does not overtly insist on asserting her classification. For the three participants some changes will have occurred during the construction of this text: the teacher may have taken some notice of the force of Aaron's argument and hence amended her classification of 'lion' somewhat; Aaron and Sarah will equally have taken note of the teacher's classification, and made adjustments to their cultural/linguistic classificatory system. Over a long time-period, in their experience of growing into culture and society (and with them, into language) they will find it difficult to sustain their classifications—they will become 'acculturated' and 'socialised'. The process as such is not a conscious one, though in the interaction the differences are made obvious and become the focus of the interaction.

Children, like all those with lesser power, are at a disadvantage: their classifications, even though they may be supported by better reasons, do not generally carry the day. For them it is a matter of falling in with the classificatory systems of those who are more powerful. That however is, as I have attempted to show, not merely a passive 'acquisition' of language, but an active (re)construction of that system in dialogue, in interaction, and in sustained resistance—which is however always a merely temporary resistance over a particular term. The process of language learning which is most congenial to my views is that of Michael Halliday in his *Learning How to Mean*. He too regards the language learner as an active participant, engaged in constructing a system of meaning-making for herself or himself, in response to interactive, social processes and demands. Although there are significant theoretical differences between Halliday's account and mine, I believe that the two are ultimately compatible in broad terms. The relevant and most significant aspects of both approaches lie, I believe, in the role given to the individual learner in the process of social and language learning. In my view the learner is active and agentive, rather than a merely passive recipient. He or she constructs the linguistic system for herself or himself in constant tension between the classifications which seem appropriate to the child at any one time and those of the larger groups into which the child is growing. Although the final outcome is that children are fully socialised into the rules, values, and meanings of their social group, the path that they have taken in travelling there leaves them situated in quite a different way than they are in a theory which regards them as merely acquiring an existent system or passively acquiescing in having a system imposed on them. In my account the language learner is always active at any stage in the process. Consequently significance attaches to everything that she or he does. Whereas within other theoretical positions it is possible to account for the child's behaviour in terms of its 'shortfall' or 'deviance' from the adult's model, and to brand that behaviour as 'error', in my account there is a need to attend carefully to the actions of the learner, for they express three crucial things at least: the child's system of classification with its cognitive, conceptual, cultural and social implications, the child's understanding of the adult systems, and the tension between these two.

Moreover, if we wish to regard the adult speaker/writer, hearer/listener as a potentially agentive participant in processes of ideological and discursive/linguistic change—as I do—we need an account

See Halliday (1975).

90

which plausibly brings him or her to that position. If we assume that language learners are essentially passive we cannot account for their activeness as mature speakers.

In my examples so far I have tried to illustrate progression and change within a single text. The most spectacular example of progression is that of individual language learners. To conclude this section I wish to illustrate progression and change in relation to genre. The three brief examples of written texts are, broadly, in the genre of scientific description. They were written by the same child at the ages of seven, twelve and fifteen respectively.

Three written texts
The Ant

The ~~ants~~ ant have a nest
under the ground.
The nest has many tunnels.
There are different kinds of ane in the nest.
There is a queen ant and male ants and worker ~~and~~ ants.

Beaked whales

(1) The Beaked Whales live out in mid-ocean, where the tasty squid are found. (2) Squid, it seems, provide most of their meals. (3) Men do not know much about their family because even the scientists who study whales have seen very few Beaked Whales. (4) Generally members of this family have long, narrow snouts, or 'beaks'. (5) They have very few teeth, just one or two on each side of the lower jaw, and these sometimes poke out like small tusks.
(6) The largest of this family is the Baird's Beaked Whale. (7) It grows to 42 ft. in length. (8) Most beaked Whales range between 15 and 30 ft. (9) The Bottlenose gets to be about 30 ft. long, and its cousin known as Cuvier's Beaked Whale grows to about 26 ft.
(10) Cuvier's Whale is rarely seen, though it is believed that it lives in all oceans. (11) It is unusual in colour so if you should see one, you should be able to recognise it. (12) Most whales have dark grey backs and pale undersides. (13) Cuvier's Beaked Whales instead has a light back and underside, and two small tusk-teeth poke up outside the mouth of the males.
(14) Bottlenose is even more odd. (15) You may possibly see one travelling in a small school of ten or twelve whales.

Here I do not wish to give a description of the three texts in terms of the development of genre or of generic features of the texts themselves. Rather I am interested how the writer is defined or placed cognitively, conceptually and socially by his relative control of the genre. The writer's use of modality differs markedly between 'The Ant' and 'Beaked Whales'. The former has the single modality of factuality or certainty expressed by the so-called universal present tense, *The ant have a nest*. The latter has a range of modalities from certainty: sentence 1 *The Beaked Whales live out in*; to a hypothetical modality: *it seems [to me and other scientific writers]* sentence 2; to a blurring, generalising modality: sentence 4 *Generally members of this family*, sentence 8 *Most*

For a discussion of the first two texts, see Kress (1982).

beaked whales; to possibility: *you should be able to recognise it*, sentence 11; to conjecture: sentence 10 *it is believed.* The difference reflects both the writer's stance *vis-à-vis* the material he is discussing, and in this, his stance *vis-à-vis* the communities in which the genres function. That is, the unidimensional modality of the first text indicates that the writer has only the single position *vis-à-vis* the material, that of description, definition, and factuality. He has neither the possibility of distancing himself from the material nor therefore the possibility of a nuanced valuation. The possibility of a differentiated stance towards the material and therefore of differentiated stances towards social groups does not arise. The multidimensional modality of the second text on the other hand indicates that the writer has a number of finely nuanced positions which he can take up *vis-à-vis* the material. The possibility of finely discriminating valuations is therefore present.

The first text is not 'addressed'; that is, no audience seems to be envisaged, or structured into the text. The reading position is identical with the writing position. The second text **is** addressed: *so if you should see one, You may possibly see.* The writing position is largely that of the anonymous scientist/writer: sentence 2 *Squid, it seems*; sentence 10 *Cuvier's whale is rarely seen, though it is believed*; though at this stage this writing position is not entirely consistently maintained. In sentence 3 the writer mentions *the scientists who study whales*, that is, he is not a member of that group. In the second text the writer has distance from the material, and also from his audience. There is thus a doubly-coded self/other distinction, which gives the writer a quite specific positioning.

In the third text the uncertainty of identification with the community defined by the genre has gone. The example here is part of a larger text of about 3500 words, with illustrative technical drawings. In each case only the opening lines of each of the four chapters are reproduced here.

Telecommunication

The electric telegraph

Before the invention of the Electric Telegraph the fastest means of conveying a message had been shouting, the speed of sound, and signalling with flags and the like. Both of these methods only good over
5 very short distances and relied on good weather conditions. The Electric Telegraph seemed instantaneous in comparison to previous methods.

Telegraphy involves completing one or more electrical circuits being completed and broken to transmit a code . . .

The telephone

10 Even though the electric telegraph was extremely fast at transmitting messages, all the messages had to be coded and sent along line one at a time with each word taking several seconds. So when the telephone came into operation it increased the speed of communication as well as making it more personal.
15 Charles Grafton Page (1812–1865) discovered, in 1837, that rapid changes in the magnetism of iron caused it to give out a musical note. Also that the pitch of the note depended on the frequence with which

these changes occurred. In 1860 Phillip Reis (1834–1874) was the first to transmit a musical melody electrically over a distance.

20 He stretched an animal membrane over a small cone to which he attached a platinum wire with sealing wax. The wire was part of an electrical circuit and when the membrane vibrated the wire completed and broke the circuit at the same frequence as the sound. At the other end of the circuit was a knitting needle with a coil of wires rapped
25 around it, and through the fact that Page had discovered the knitting needle reproduced the sound. Three years later he claimed 'that words can also be made out'. . .

The radio or wireless

The telegraph and telephone had revolutionised communication but they
30 both had one big drawback in that they couldn't be used to communicate with moving vehicles such as trains or boats.
The story of radio perhaps begins with Joseph Henry (1779–1878) who, in 1842, showed that electrical discharges were oscillations. . .

The television

35 The first developments of the television came at about the same time as the radio, but it took much long to develop than the radio . . .

The writer is fully in control of the genre. It is a multimodal text: line 7 *Telegraphy involves completing*, and line 32 *The story of radio perhaps begins*; line 10 *Even though the electric telegraph was extremely*; line 5–6 *The electric telegraph seemed instantaneous*; line 26 *Three years later he claimed*. These clearly indicate the writer's stance towards his material and towards his audience; and he now writes as a member of the scientific community. Within this he establishes his own writing position, for instance most obviously in line 32 *The story of radio perhaps begins* where *perhaps* indicates his own careful judgment; or lines 5–6 *The Electric Telegraph seemed instantaneous in comparison.*

The modalities of 'The Ant' text suggest a world of certainty, certain because no questions as yet arise for the writer, in which the writer is at one with what he is writing. The modalities of the third text suggest a complex world, made up of some certainties, some generally-accepted hypotheses, historically given 'facts', and carefully made personal valuations. In each of the two texts the individual has a specific positioning: as an unself-conscious individual in the first, and as a highly self-conscious member of a complex of social groupings in the second.

The linguistic system and time

There are, as I mentioned at the outset of this chapter, very many aspects of this topic which I will not be able to discuss. For instance, in many texts one or both participants actively resist change—as in the case where a politician resists the pressing of an interviewer to shift his or her position over some problematic matter, or to concede a point in a contentious area. Advertisers may not wish to imply any change in their product, so that a McEagleburger is always a McEagleburger and texts are constructed to assert this. Conservative politics—at whatever level— are about texts of this kind. However, such texts still bear the obligatory signs of 'progression', however superficial.

One aspect which I will address very briefly is the effect of individual action on the discursive and generic system overall. Imagine that because of her or his social positioning a speaker is placed in such a way that she or he uses a certain set of discourses, sexist discourse included. Because of that social positioning he or she also tends to assume specific roles in interactions and in texts, let us assume, the roles which are always the less powerful. There is therefore an habitual, though socially-determined, conjunction of a certain subject position and certain textual and reading positions. That conjunction determines the use of certain forms of language. Over time that habitual use becomes codified, and then becomes a code.

To make this concrete: sexist discourse suggests subject positions for women. That is, it suggests to women to be and to act in certain ways, to relate to others in a particular manner, and so on. This will strongly shape the kinds of language a woman will use or that will be used about women. Assume further that the woman, by the effects of class and gender is habitually placed in certain ways in genres, for instance, generally not to be a committee member, let alone the chairperson; not usually to be interviewer but interviewee in say, an interview in the doctor's surgery; not to be the professional; but to be engaged in household labour, to be patronised by all, to be always a part of the world of the private and not to have a public role. Her modes of speaking clearly will be shaped by this experience. If the situation persists, the mode of speaking will become habitual and 'natural' for her. If the situation is one where many speakers are involved, the same general kinds of texts will be being produced on many occasions. A recognisably distinct manner of speaking, a new code, will have emerged. New speakers will grow into a situation where the code already exists as the usual, the 'natural' or even the 'proper' way for women to talk. In this way a code is established by individuals acting as social agents in time, whose actions are nevertheless always socially conditioned.

In much the same way modes of talking can become altered. The theoretical analyses of feminist writers, and the social practices of feminists over a long period are bringing about a recognisable change in the discourses around gender, and in social practices.

Language, time and education

Social systems are complex, and language is no exception. Furthermore, these systems are constantly in process, in tension, constantly open to challenge and change. In the attempt to understand the complexities of any system there is always not only the temptation but also the need to generalise and to abstract, and thereby to think of the system itself abstractly or as an abstraction, out of time and out of context. The process is entirely understandable; the result is invariably a falsification. Throughout this little book I have suggested that language has to be seen as one social system in interaction with other social systems, in constant process, and in time. The major theoretical paradoxes then disappear: we can see that at any one point language has autonomy and yet that in time and in use it is constantly intermeshed with all other social systems, which exert their effect on language. We can understand how in the speaker's own personal time language exerts its rules and classifications and yet how at any one moment the individual is agentive in the construction of texts in relation to language change.

In thinking about language there are different kinds of time, which apply in differing ways. We know that languages change, and that the language of Shakespeare is noticeably different from the language of Australians in the 1980s. We vaguely perceive that older generations use language differently to the way we do: sometimes that realisation emerges as an irritation about the other's speech, as excessively 'slangy' or as unnecessarily deliberate and quaintly constructed. We know that differing groups use differing 'jargons'; counter-cultural groups of every generation create distinctive forms of language only to find their forms reincorporated into the mainstream by fashion-conscious mainstream speakers. We know that in some of the interactions that we have participated in things did not go the way we wanted, that we could have put things better, or said things more clearly. In other words, in some exchange constructed around discursive difference, the course of the interaction did not favour our position. All these are examples of language in time and in (social) process. These different times move at quite different rates, with different momentum and energy. At times certain tendencies merge, and permanent changes occur.

What is important is to think of language always as a complex system, in movement, sometimes contradictory and sometimes in a single direction. In all of these processes the individual is crucial and instrumental. Education is that social institution which is about the change and progression of its client members in the direction of mainstream culture, and into its classifications. The institution of education absolutely depends on a theory of language in which notions of change and progression are at the centre.

References

Barthes, R., 'The death of the author', in S. Heath (ed.), *Image Music Text* (Fontana, Glasgow, 1977).

Belsey, C., *Critical Practice* (Methuen, London, 1980).

Bennett, T., 'Texts in History: The determinations of readings and their texts', in P. Widdowson (ed.), *Re-reading English* (Methuen, London, 1982).

Benterrak, K., Muecke, S., & Roe, P. *Reading the Country* (Fremantle Arts Centre Press, Fremantle, Western Australia, 1984).

Brown, R., & Gilman, A., 'The pronouns of power and solidarity', in T. Sebeok (ed.), *Style in Language* (MIT Press, Cambridge, Massachusetts, 1960).

Christie, F., 'Writing in schools, generic structures as ways of meaning.' Mimeographed paper (School of Education, Deakin University, Victoria, 1984).

Christie, M.J., *Aboriginal Perspectives on Experience and Learning: The Role of Language in Aboriginal Education*, ECS 806 Sociocultural Aspects of Language and Education (Deakin University, Geelong, Victoria, 1985).

Downes, W., *Language and Society* (Fontana, London, 1984).

Fasold, R., *The Sociolinguistics of Society* (Blackwell, Oxford, 1984).

Foucault, M., 'What is an author?', in D. Bouchard (ed.), *Language, Counter-Memory, Practice* (Cornell University Press, Ithaca, New York, 1977).

Fowler, R., Hodge, R.I.V., Kress, G., & Trew, T., *Language and Control* (Routledge and Kegan Paul, London, 1979).

Halliday, M.A.K., *Learning How to Mean: Explorations in the Development of Language* (Edward Arnold, London, 1975).

Halliday, M.A.K., *Language as Social Semiotic: The Social Interpretation of Language and Meaning* (Edward Arnold, London, 1978).

Halliday, M.A.K., *Spoken and Written Language* (Oxford University Press, Oxford, 1989).

Hymes, D., 'Models of the interaction of language and social life', in J. Gumperz & D.Hymes (eds.), *Directions in Sociolinguistics: The Ethnography of Communication* (Holt, Rinehart & Winston, New York, 1972).

Hymes, D., *Foundations in Sociolinguistics: An Ethnographic Approach* (University of Pennsylvania Press, Philadelphia, 1974).

Kress, G.R. (ed.), *Halliday: Systems and Function in Language* (Oxford University Press, London, 1976).

Kress, G.R., *Learning to Write* (Routledge and Kegan Paul, London, 1982).

Kress, G.R., & Hodge, R.I.V., *Language as Ideology* (Routledge and Kegan Paul, London, 1979).

Lakoff, G., & Johnson, M., *Metaphors We Live By* (University of Chicago Press, Chicago, 1980).

Martin, J.R., *Factual Writing: Exploring and Challenging Social Reality* (Oxford University Press, Oxford, 1989).

Norris, C.H., *Deconstruction* (Methuen, London, 1982).

Poynton, C., *Language and Gender: Making the Difference* (Oxford University Press, Oxford, 1989).

Roe, P., *gularabulu* (Fremantle Arts Centre Press, Fremantle, Western Australia, 1982).

Saussure, F. de. *Course in General Linguistics*, ed. C. Bally & A. Sechehaye in collaboration with A. Reidlinger, tr. W. Baskin (McGraw-Hill, New York, 1966).

Saville-Troike, M., *The Ethnography of Communication* (Blackwell, Oxford, 1982).

Sinclair, J., & Coulthard, M., *Towards an Analysis of Discourse* (Oxford University Press, London, 1975).

Spender, D., *Invisible Women* (Writers and Readers, London, 1982).

Spender, D., *Man made Language* (Routledge & Kegan Paul, London, 1980).

Thorne, B., Kramare, C.H., & Henley, N. (eds.), *Language, Gender and Society*, Newbury House, Rowley, Massachusetts, 1983).

Further reading

A brief discussion of the titles listed below is provided to help guide your reading.

Barthes, R., 'The death of the author', in S. Heath (ed.), *Image Music Text* (Fontana, Glasgow, 1977).
Belsey. C., *Critical Practice* (Methuen, London, 1980).
Downes, W., *Language and Society* (Fontana, London, 1984).
Fasold, R., *The Sociolinguistics of Society* (Blackwell, Oxford, 1984).
Hymes, D., 'Models of the interaction of language and social life', in J. Gumperz & D.Hymes (eds.), *Directions in Sociolinguistics: The Ethnography of Communication* (Holt, Rinehart & Winston, New York, 1972).
Hymes, D., *Foundations in Sociolinguistics: An Ethnographic Approach* (University of Pennsylvania Press, Philadelphia, 1974).
Norris, C.H., *Deconstruction* (Methuen, London, 1982).
Saville-Troike, M., *The Ethnography of Communication* (Blackwell, Oxford, 1982).
Spender, D., *Invisible Women* (Writers and Readers, London, 1982).
Spender, D., *Man made Language* (Routledge & Kegan Paul, London, 1980).
Thorne, D., Kramare, C.H., & Henley, N., (eds.), *Language, Gender and Society* (Newbury House, Rowley, Massachusetts, 1983).

My argument is in many ways, and by design, a departure from a more traditional linguistic approach. Perhaps it will help to characterise the latter in a few sentences. Within the discipline of linguistics there is a strong and still largely dominant strand which regards the study of phonology and syntax and their theoretical treatment as 'real' linguistics. This strand asserts the autonomy of linguistics, in terms of its theories, methodologies and subject matter. The approach is characterised in journals such as *Language, Journal of Linguistics, Linguistic Inquiry.* In the late 1950s, 1960s and 1970s, this approach was epitomised by the work of Noam Chomsky and of the theory of Transformational Grammar. Another strand has always emphasised the social dimensions of language. In England in the 1920s and 1930s, this was particularly emphasised in the work of the anthropologist Bronislaw

Malinowski and the linguist J. R. Firth. The theoretical work of Michael Halliday is in that tradition. In the mid-1960s, the American linguist Dell Hymes introduced the concept of 'communicative competence' in reaction to Chomsky's narrow and asocial definition of linguistic competence. Hymes's work has been most important both as a corrective and an alternative theory of language as a social phenomenon. He is founder and editor of the journal *Language in Society* in which work of that kind appears. I should mention here too the work of William Labov. Although I myself have misgivings about the theoretical (and ideological) basis of his research, it establishes the relation of linguistic and social matters in an empirically unassailable manner. His later development of variation theory is one mode of conceptualising the complexities, tensions and shifts of language difference within a society. Bill Downes's *Language and Society* makes much use of his theory. It will serve as an introduction to that work, but beyond that it is a careful and thoughtful book within the mainstream of sociolinguistic writing. Muriel Saville-Troike's *The Ethnography of Communication* is written more within Dell Hymes's broad framework. It too is thoughtful and stimulating. Ralph Fasold's *The Sociolinguistics of Society* is Labovian in orientation; I have included it in the further reading because it has much to say about languages in interaction, a topic of obvious importance in multi-ethnic, multi-cultural Australia.

One significant strand in my own thinking is that of structuralism and of semiotics. These traditions are broad, and diffuse. Semiotics has been useful to me because it regards all human activity as systematically meaningful. Hence it provides a larger perspective not only on 'extra-linguistic' activity and its meanings, but also gives a much more searching perspective on linguistic activity itself. Roland Barthes's *Image Music Text* is a collection of very readable essays in a semiotic and structuralist vein. Catherine Belsey's *Critical Practice* is (post-) structuralist. I have found this tradition useful because unlike the speaker/production-centred approach of all linguistic theories, structuralist accounts, in paying attention to all elements of a structure, give equal prominence, for instance, to the reader/consumer, and provide a thorough revaluation of the notion of 'reading'. Christopher Norris's *Deconstruction* is a book in that tradition.

In my discussion I have made much use of feminist analyses of sexist discourse. Although I find some of her arguments asserted rather than demonstrated, Dale Spender's *Invisible Women* provides convincing support in most areas for the general arguments about the effects of sexist discourse on women. Her earlier (1980) *Man made Language* is an attempt to show the origins and present reproductive mechanisms of sexist discourse, or rather, of English as a sexist language. My own views are quite different here, in that I would give much more emphasis to general factors such as class, and power difference. A recent collection of articles by Barrie Thorne, Nancy Henley and Cheris Kramare, *Language and Gender*, provides a broad survey and contains an extensive annotated bibliography.

Technical Terms

Acknowledgements

The author and publishers would like to thank the following for permission to reproduce the material below:

p. 10 and 71   Extract from *Survival: Man and his World Book 4* by K. L. Marriott, P. J. Palmer, B. Raufer, G. K. Thompson, and E. Vlass. Reproduced by permission of Macmillan Co. of Australia.

p. 58 and 79   Letter/memorandum—Education Department of S.A., 1970. Reproduced by permission.

p. 66   Extract from 'Duegara' in *Gularabulu: Stories from the West Kimberley* by Paddy Roe (editor Stephen Muecke), published by Fremantle Arts Centre Press, 1983.

p. 68   © S. B. Codrington and D. M. Codrington. Reprinted from *World of Contrasts* by permission of William Brooks & Co., Sydney.